WITHDRAWN

Still Running

Children on the Streets in the UK

SAFE ON THE STREETS RESEARCH TEAM

Research Director
Professor Mike Stein, University of York

Research Coordinator
Gwyther Rees, The Children's Society

Researchers

Lorraine Wallis
Jim Wade
Myfanwy Franks
Joanne Stevenson

Saira Mumtaz
Dee Lynes
Liz Johnson
Phil Raws

Field Interviewers

Emilie Smeaton
Kay Sayer
Mandana Hendessi
Anne du Chemin
Amanda Durlik

Bolaji Bank-Anthony
Caroline McAuley
Val Williams
David Williams

Administrative Support

Sue Borwell
Andrea Brown

Helen Whiteley
Joyce Watt

D1395747

The Children's Society

A Voluntary Society of The Church of England and The Church in Wales

First published in 1999

The Children's Society
Edward Rudolf House
Margery Street
London WC1X 0JL

A catalogue record of this book is available from
the British Library.

ISBN 1 899783 31 8

Acknowledgements
The authors would like to thank the young people and
professionals who made the research possible by contributing
their views and experiences.

   The Children's Society would like to thank the members
of the Publications Advisory Group for their valued advice:
Kathy Aubeelack; Nicola Baboneau; Ron Chopping (Chair);
Annabelle Dixon; Sara Fielden; Judy Foster; Christopher Walsh.

Cover photograph modelled for The Children's Society.

Contents

List of tables

Foreword

I am pleased to introduce this authoritative new report which presents a vivid picture of the lives of some of the most excluded young people in UK society. Reading the report, and reflecting on the issues it highlights, provoked in me a number of reactions.

First, I was surprised at the extent of the problem of young people running away in the UK. The research estimates that there are at least 129,000 incidents of young people under 16 running away each year, and that the phenomenon affects one in nine young people. These figures are alarmingly high for one of the more prosperous countries of the world, with a well-developed social welfare system.

I was also struck by the disturbing universality of the research findings on the causes and consequences of running away – the abuse, rejection and neglect which lead many young people to run away; the dangers and risks of exploitation which they may face while away; and the poverty, powerlessness and exclusion which young people can experience if they become detached from their carers and communities. These are experiences which resonate with those of street children around the world.

The findings of the research are yet another reminder of the relevance that the UN Convention on the Rights of the Child has for disadvantaged and vulnerable children and young people in all countries. The three key themes of the Convention are protection, provision and participation. The young people described in this report are very much in need of both better protection and improved provision. However, they are also both willing and able to participate. This potential comes across powerfully in the many quotes from young people throughout the report. In particular I was impressed by the depth and quality of the comments from young people when asked for their ideas about what should be done to help young runaways, presented in the penultimate chapter of the report. These comments are further evidence, if any is needed, of the value of actively involving children and young people in the processes and systems which affect their lives.

The scale of the problem, and the evidence on the experiences of young people whilst away, supports the persuasive case which the report makes for the need for an urgent response at both the practice and policy levels. I believe that the research presented in this report is a major step forward in understanding the issue of young people running away. As such, it carries important messages from which we can learn much about improving the lives of children and young people both in the UK and in other countries.

E. M. Q. MOKHUANE
Vice Chairperson,
Committee on the Rights of the Child,
United Nations

Editorial preface

One of The Children's Society's national programmes of work aims to provide a safety net for runaways and young people at risk on the street. This work forms the Society's commitment to the Children's Promise, a nationwide appeal backed by Marks & Spencer and the New Millennium Company. The research in this report forms one element of the Children's Promise programme of work and has been planned jointly by The Children's Society, Aberlour Child Care Trust and the EXTERN Organisation. It is the fourth in a series of research studies which The Children's Society has published over the last decade into the issue of young people running away.

The Children's Society's involvement in this area of work stretches back to 1985 when it set up the first ever refuge in the UK for young people under the age of 18 who had run away from home, the Central London Teenage Project. The work of this project featured in the *Young Runaways* research report published in 1989.

The Society was subsequently at the forefront of a successful campaign to incorporate provision for such refuges in the Children Act 1989. At around the same time, the Society set up a number of refuge and streetwork projects for runaways. More recently some of these projects have begun to pilot and develop strategies aimed at preventing young people from having to run away or live on the streets. The Society then went on to publish two further research reports about young runaways – *Hidden Truths* in 1993 and *Running – the Risk* in 1994 – both of which added significantly to our knowledge about young people in this situation.

The Children's Society's work in this area led to the Game's Up campaign. The campaign was successful in initiating government guidelines with regard to young people sexually abused through prostitution, ensuring that child prostitution is seen as a child protection issue in the first instance. The Society recently commissioned a retrospective study of people involved in prostitution as children, *One Way Street?*, to develop our understanding of routes into and out of prostitution.

The Children's Society remains at the forefront of innovative work with this vulnerable group of young people, in terms of both practice and research. It is hoped that the current research will point the way forward for the further development of such work within all organisations, both statutory and voluntary, concerned with young people who run away from home or care.

The current research is a joint venture between four organisations. Funding and resources for the research have been provided jointly by The Children's Society (in England and Wales), Aberlour Child Care Trust (in Scotland) and the EXTERN Organisation (in Northern Ireland). The research has been planned and undertaken in partnership with the Department of Social Policy and Social Work at the University of York.

PENNY DEAN
Programme Manager,
The Children's Society

PART *1*

The background to the study

CHAPTER 1

Introduction

This report focuses on the issue of young people under 18 running away from or being forced to leave where they live. It presents the results of a national needs analysis, carried out in early 1999, which gathered information from over 13,000 young people and over 400 agencies in 27 different areas of the UK. Whilst there have been several important research studies into young people running away over the last decade in the UK, this is the first report which can claim to portray an overall picture of the issue. The scale of the research has made it possible for the first time to arrive at reasonable estimates of the incidence of running away amongst young people under 16, and has provided substantial new insights into the phenomenon.

The research shows that there are large numbers of young people in the UK who run away or are forced to leave home before the age of 18. In some cases, this is a short-term situation; in other cases it becomes a semi-permanent way of life. Whilst there is considerable diversity amongst these young people, the research illustrates that there are a number of recurring themes in their experiences which are similar. These include: family instability, conflict, violence, abuse, neglect, rejection, drug problems, and problems at school. Many of these issues link to a central theme of the report, that of social exclusion.

Through gathering together the experiences and views of thousands of young people and hundreds of professionals who work with them, we have been able to trace some of the causes of young people running away as well as some of the consequences. The evidence presented in this report represents a challenge to all those involved with children and young people, whether as parents, practitioners, or policy makers. As we will conclude, there is a range of actions which can be taken by people in all these roles to prevent young people from running away and to support young people who do spend time away from home. These young people are amongst the most marginalised and excluded members of our society.

DEFINITIONS

One challenge faced by this research relates to definitions: what do we mean by young people 'running away'? This is an issue that previous research has also dealt with and a variety of other terms are also in common usage, e.g. 'going missing', 'on the streets', 'absconding', 'thrown out', 'homeless', 'travellers', 'sofa surfing', and so on. It is clear from previous research that, whilst 'running away' is perhaps the most commonly used phrase, some young people are literally forced to leave home rather than choosing to leave.

For this research, we are concerned with two groups of young people:

1. Young people who are:

   • under 16;

   • aged 16 to 17 and 'looked after' by the local authority;

   and who spend time away from home or substitute care either without permission ('running away') or having been forced to leave by their parents or carers.

2. Young people aged 16 or 17 who are not in one of the above groups and spend time away from a stable place to live (whether this is with parents, in a hostel, or independent accommodation).

The reason for drawing a distinction between the two groups stems from the differing legal position of the two groups, as we discuss later in this introduction. This also accounts for the sub-groups within the first group.

We will use the term 'running away' to encapsulate the act of leaving home for young people in the above situations. Where there is a need for greater precision, we may make a distinction between those who run away and those who are forced to leave. We will use the term 'being away' to describe young people's situation whilst they are away from stable accommodation in any of the above contexts.

We have kept our area of interest as broad as possible in a conscious attempt to explore the meaning of 'running away' from young people's and professionals' perspectives, rather than to predefine it. In this report we will attempt to reflect the diversity of meanings which running away can have for different young people in different contexts.

The above definition does not stipulate a minimum duration for a running away incident. Our main focus in the report will be on young people who have spent at least one night away from home whilst in one of the above situations. Unless otherwise stated, all statistics in the report relate to young people with this experience. However, as we will see in Chapter 8, the incidence and significance of young people running away during the day should not be underestimated.

Throughout the report we use the term 'young people' to refer to all those under the age of 18.

PREVIOUS RESEARCH

In the UK in the last two decades there has been much research activity regarding young people running away. As we refer regularly to this research during the report, a brief overview is provided here.

Table 1.1 summarises the main studies, the research methods and sampling strategies used. Each of the studies focused on a specific sub-sample of the total population of young people running away (e.g. young people reported as missing, young people using a service for runaways, young people in a certain location or environment). Thus, none of the studies can claim to present an overall picture of the issue. Nevertheless, this body of research has produced a range of findings, some conclusive and others more tentative, which have informed the debate about young people running away and have guided the development of services.

It should also be noted that there is a substantial amount of research literature on running away in the USA, going back more than two decades. We do not review this literature here, but refer at various points in the report to a key study by Brennan *et al.* (1978) which, despite its age, provides a valuable overview of the phenomenon.

Table 1.1 *Previous UK research into young people who run away or are forced to leave home*

Author, year, title and publisher	Research methods	Sample
1 Newman (1989) *Young Runaways: Findings from Britain's First Safe House.* The Children's Society	Secondary data analysis of missing persons reports	Police authorities in England and Wales
	Interviews with young people	Young people staying in refuge in London
2 Abrahams and Mungall (1992) *Young Runaways: Exploding the Myths.* NCH Action for Children	Secondary data analysis of missing persons reports	Five selected police authorities in England and Scotland
3 Rees (1993) *Hidden Truths: Young People's Experiences of Running Away.* The Children's Society	Questionnaire survey of young people	Sample of young people aged 14 to 16 in Leeds
	Interviews with young people	Young people staying in refuge in Leeds
4 Stein *et al.* (1994) *Running – the Risk: Young People on the Streets of Britain Today.* The Children's Society	Questionnaires and interviews with young people and professionals	Young people under 18 using four projects aimed at young runaways in Birmingham, Leeds, Manchester and Newport
5 Barter (1996) *Nowhere to Hide: Giving Young Runaways a Voice.* Centrepoint/NSPCC	Interviews with young people	Young people staying in refuge in London

| 6 Wade *et al.* (1998) *Going Missing: Young People Absent from Care.* Wiley | Questionnaire and interviews with young people and professionals | Young people running away from care in four local authority areas |

Some of the key findings from the previous research are given below. Numbers in brackets refer to the numbered references in Table 1.1.

PREVALENCE AND CHARACTERISTICS

- In 1990, an estimated 43,000 young people under the age of 18 were reported missing in England and Scotland. [2]

- An estimated one in seven young people in Leeds run away overnight at least once before the age of 16. [3]

- Females are more likely to run away than males. [1], [3]

- Young people of African-Caribbean origin are more likely than average to run away. Those of Asian origin are less likely than average to run away. [2], [3]

CONTEXT AND TRIGGERS

- Problematic family backgrounds, including physical, sexual and emotional abuse, are the most common contexts in which running away takes place, and most young people run away because of these problems. [1], [3], [4], [5]

- Young people who live in substitute care are particularly likely to be reported missing. [1], [2] They also seem to be more likely to run away. [3] Young people's histories, including both family factors and substitute care experiences, combine to contribute to this incidence of running away.[6]

- There are links between running away and non-attendance at school. [3], [6]

- There is some evidence that young people who repeatedly run away have higher than average problems with depression, alcohol, drugs and offending. [4], [6]

Experiences of being away

- Most young people who run away do so only once or twice. [3]

- Many young people sleep rough whilst away from home. [3]

- Very few young people approach agencies for help or advice whilst they are away, although friends and relatives are often used as means of support. [3]

- Few young people go outside their local area whilst away. [2]

- Young people who run away repeatedly often report being frightened and lonely whilst away, and some are physically or sexually assaulted. [4]

- There are also often some positive aspects to being away for young people, including respite from problems and making new friends. [4]

- Most young people return home of their own accord. [3], [6]

Key gaps in knowledge from the previous research

As already discussed, one of the drawbacks with all of the previous research has been its focus on specific sub-groups of young people. In addition, despite the knowledge that has been accumulated, there are some major gaps in the knowledge base from this research:

- There are no reliable estimates of the prevalence of running away throughout the UK.

- There is no representative picture of the reasons for running away of young people who only run away once or twice.

- Very little knowledge is available about running away in rural areas and there is only limited information for suburban areas. Most of the focus has been on large cities.

- Little is known about the reasons for running away or experiences whilst away for young people of African-Caribbean and Indian/Pakistani/Bangladeshi origin.

One of the aims of the current research was to fill these gaps in our understanding of young people running away or being forced to leave where they live.

THE LEGAL POSITION OF YOUNG PEOPLE UNDER 18 WHO ARE AWAY FROM HOME

In this section, we discuss the legal position of young people aged under 18 who are away from home without parental permission. This position is rather complicated and in a state of flux. We therefore attempt only to provide a broad picture to the extent that is necessary for the purposes of the report. We divide the discussion into two age groups – under 16 and 16 to 17 – and discuss, for both groups, their legal status and the options open to them whilst away from home.

THE LEGAL POSITION OF YOUNG PEOPLE AWAY FROM HOME UNDER THE AGE OF 16

Legal status whilst away

It is an offence for someone to 'harbour' or to abduct a child under 16 who has left home (Section 49 of the Children Act 1989; Section 83 of the Children (Scotland) Act 1995; the Children (Northern Ireland) Order 1995; Section 71 of the Social Work (Scotland) Act 1968; Section 32(3) of the Children and Young Persons Act 1969; Section 2 of the Child Abduction Act 1984). It is also common practice for the police to return a young runaway to her or his parents or carers.

If a young person wants to leave home under 16, they may under certain circumstances apply through formal court proceedings (under the Children Act 1989 in England and Wales, The Children (Scotland) Act 1995 or the Children (Northern Ireland) Order 1995) for a Residence Order to substitute parental responsibility with that of another acceptable adult who can take parental responsibility for them.

In general, then, it is not legally possible for a young person under the age of 16 to choose to leave home and they are likely to be returned home if they are found.

There is, however, one key exception to the above principle. There is provision in England, Wales, Northern Ireland and Scotland for the setting up of refuges which are exempt from the laws on harbouring and which can accommodate, for a short period, young people under 16 who have run away. The relevant provisions are contained in Section 51 of the Children Act 1989, Section 38 of the Children (Scotland) Act 1995, and Article 70 of the Children (Northern Ireland) Order

1995. In England and Wales such refuges can accommodate young people for up to 14 days in a continuous period and for no more than 21 days in any three-month period. In Scotland, the time limit is seven days, or 14 days in exceptional circumstances.

Since the introduction of the Children Act 1989, four refuges have been set up in England and Wales (three by The Children's Society and one by the NSPCC and Centrepoint working in partnership). However, currently only two refuges are in operation, one in Leeds and the other in London, and each can only accommodate a very limited number of young people at any time (six in Leeds and 12 in London). So far, no refuges have been set up in Scotland. Thus whilst there is legal provision for refuges for under-16s, the reality is that, for most young people who run away, this is not an option.

Options open to young people under 16 whilst away
Young people under the age of 16 have no entitlements to any welfare benefits, have only limited ability to work, should be still at school, and cannot enter into contracts to obtain independent accommodation. They therefore have no legitimate means either of supporting themselves or living independently whilst away.

Other notes
In terms of young people under 16 being away from home, 'being beyond parental control' is one of the grounds of referral to the Reporter to the Children's Hearing (Children) Scotland Act 1995, and this can include young people who run away. 'Any person', including a police officer or parent, can refer. This is not emergency legislation.

One other noteworthy difference in the legislation for this age group is that it is only in Scotland that there is a general requirement for parents to take into account children's views in reaching any decisions affecting them (Section 6 of the Children (Scotland) Act 1995).

THE LEGAL POSITION OF YOUNG PEOPLE AWAY FROM HOME AT 16 AND 17

The position of 16- and 17-year-olds who are away from home is much more complex both in terms of their status and the options open to them.

Legal status whilst away

In England, Wales and Northern Ireland, the legal status of 16- and 17-year-olds regarding being away from home is the same as for the under-16 age group discussed above. Usually they may not leave home without parental permission, the laws on 'harbouring' apply, and police will normally return young runaways to their home if they find them. In practice, however, with the exception of young people being looked after at this age, this law is more a technicality than a reality. It would be extremely unusual for the police to return young people to their parents against their will or for a person or organisation to be prosecuted for 'harbouring' them. For young people being looked after, however, it is not uncommon for the police to use their powers to return young people to their carers, and their situation is more akin to under-16s.

In Scotland, the situation is different. There is no specific legislation in relation to young people being able to leave home at 16. Rather, it stems from the legal definition of a child, who is someone under 16 or subject to statutory supervision in terms of Section 70 of the 1995 Children (Scotland) Act. Anyone who is not a child is an adult, and therefore able to leave home legally.

Options open to young people aged 16 and 17 whilst away

Whilst the options open to 16- and 17-year-olds in terms of income and housing when they are away from home are quite limited in comparison with people aged 18 and over, they are also considerably more extensive than those for under-16s.

First, in terms of income, young people are legally allowed to leave school at or soon after the age of 16 (Section 9 Education Act 1962 as amended by Education (School-leaving Dates) Act 1976) and can work full time if they have left school (Section 58 Education Act 1944). In addition, in some circumstances, young people of this age may obtain welfare benefits in the form of severe hardship payments for limited periods whilst they are away from home, although these payments are discretionary. They may also receive benefits if in education or training. However, even where young people do receive benefits, these are at a lower level than for people aged 18 and over. Entitlement to housing benefit is not discretionary, so any 16- or 17-year-old who is independently accommodated can make a claim, although often this will not cover all of their housing costs.

Second, in terms of housing, there are additional options available to this age group. In particular, hostels can accommodate 16- and 17-year-olds without parental permission without fear of being prosecuted for 'harbouring' them. An exception to this is in Northern Ireland, where the usual lower age limit for hostels is 17 rather than 16. In practice, most large cities and many smaller population centres throughout the UK have hostels which will accommodate young people in this age group. Many of these hostels are run by non-statutory sector organisations and often they cater specifically for the 16 to 21 or to 25 age groups. Thus, there are many more short-term bed spaces available to 16- and 17-year-olds than the 18 that exist for young people under the age of 16.

Other accommodation options are still very limited for this age group, however. Young people aged 16 and 17 are generally not auto-matically accepted under the homelessness legislation in any of the four nations, with the exception of young people who are looked after by a local authority at school-leaving age, or later in Scotland. Local authorities may accommodate young people of this age who are 'at risk' without the permission of parents, but again this is a discre-tionary power and its implementation varies in different areas. Local authorities also have a duty under the Children Act 1989 Section 20(3) to accommodate 16- to 17-year-olds who are considered to be children in need. Young people of this age are also generally not given a tenancy by a local authority unless there is an adult who will act as guarantor for the rent. Technically, also, young people of this age may not enter into a legal contract. This would preclude accom-modation in the private-rented sector, although in practice this does sometimes happen.

SUMMARY OF THE LEGAL SITUATION

In summary, the options open to young people under the age of 18 who are away from home are quite limited. Young people under the age of 16 have no means of housing or supporting themselves independently. For many 16- and 17-year-olds, a wider range of options is available, including hostel accommodation and access to some benefits. How-ever, young people in this age group have far fewer options than adults and face considerable obstacles in establishing legitimate independent financial and housing status.

THE STRUCTURE OF THE REPORT

The differences that we have described in the legal position of young people under 16 and those over 16 affected the way that the research was conducted with these two age groups. The analysis of the research and the differences between the two age groups also influenced the structure of this report. The report is divided into four parts.

Part 1 gives the background to the study and consists of this introductory chapter and Chapter 2, which describes the research methodology.

Part 2 has six chapters and presents the research findings on young people running away from or being forced to leave home under the age of 16. Chapter 3 presents evidence on the prevalence of running away and the characteristics of young runaways. Chapter 4 looks at the immediate reasons for young people running away or being forced to leave. Chapters 5 and 6 consider the home and wider contexts which form the backdrop to young people running away from home. Chapter 7 looks at young people's experiences whilst away from home and examines the question of whether there is a developing pattern of running away. Chapter 8 describes different sub-groups of runaways and provides some illustrative case studies.

Part 3 presents the research findings on young people being away from home at the ages of 16 and 17. It follows a similar format to Part 2. Chapter 9 looks at prevalence and characteristics. Chapter 10 examines the contexts and triggers which lead to young people being away. Chapter 11 describes young people's experiences whilst away from home. Chapter 12 identifies some sub-groups of young people who spend time away at this age, again making use of case studies.

Part 4 consists of two chapters. Chapter 13 summarises suggestions from young people and from professionals about what should be done to prevent young people from running away or having to leave home. It also discusses what should be done to help young people who are away from home. Chapter 14 concludes the report with a summary of key findings and the identification of social policy issues and potential practice responses.

CHAPTER 2

Research methods

AIMS

The aims of the research were agreed as follows:
  • to estimate the prevalence and characteristics of young people under 18 running away, being forced to leave home, and/or being on the streets;

  • to learn more about patterns of running away and/or being on the streets including reasons, circumstances, events whilst away/on the streets, and returning home;

  • to identify the potential needs of the young people in the target group and to explore appropriate responses to these needs.

BROAD METHODS

A key factor in selecting the most appropriate methods for carrying out the research was the tight timescale, and this led to the selection of methods which had already proved to be feasible in previous research projects with disadvantaged young people.

The two key elements of the research were as follows:

1. A survey with the aim of quantifying the extent of being away from home amongst young people under the age of 16, identifying characteristics of young people who run away, and learning more about their reasons for running away and experiences whilst away.

2. An exploration of the meaning and nature of being 'on the streets' under the age of 18, gathering the experiences and views of young people and professionals who work with them.

When put together, these two elements would enable the research to meet the specified aims.

SAMPLING

It was decided to divide resources equally between the two elements of the research. This meant that it was possible to carry out a survey in around 25 areas of the UK and to conduct qualitative interviewing of young people and professionals in about half of these areas. Within these constraints, a primary consideration in making sampling decisions was the need to reflect the diversity of young people in the four countries which make up the UK.

Given the relative population sizes of the four countries, it was decided to conduct the survey in 16 areas in England, and three areas each in Northern Ireland, Scotland and Wales, and to carry out interviews in eight areas of England and two areas each in the other three countries.

THE SAMPLE IN ENGLAND

In England, stratified random sampling was used to select the areas for the research. In order to be able to arrive at accurate estimates of the incidence of running away by means of the survey, the country was divided into eight types of area, and two areas were randomly selected from each stratum.

An important factor in selecting the strata was to ensure that young people of different ethnic origins were adequately represented in the final sample. This was an issue both in terms of reflecting diversity and because previous research had suggested that there were significant variations in rates of running away for young people of different origins. A second important consideration was to ensure that rural and suburban areas were adequately represented. As noted earlier, previous research had tended to focus mainly on cities.

Data from the 1991 Census (OPCS, 1994) indicated that the bulk of the population of people of ethnic minority origin was concentrated in a relatively small number of areas of England. Two strata were constructed solely from these areas. Stratum 1 consisted of those areas where the proportion of people of African-Caribbean origin was greater than 10%. This stratum made up around 5% of the total population of England. Stratum 2 consisted of those areas not already allocated to Stratum 1 where the proportion of people of Indian, Pakistani and Bangladeshi origin was greater than 10%. This stratum made up a further 10% of the total population of England. The remaining areas were divided into three groups according to population density, and each of these groups was divided into two strata according to indicators of economic prosperity. The resulting six strata were of approximately equal size, each containing around 14% of the total population of England. Two areas were then randomly selected from each of the eight strata with probabilities proportional to the size of the population of young people in the area.

The resulting sample areas are shown in Table 2.1 and Figure 2.1.

Table 2.1 *Areas and strata from which the sample in England was taken*

Strata	Areas selected	
High %age of young people of African-Caribbean origin	Lambeth	Hackney
High %age of young people of Indian/Pakistani/Bangladeshi origin	Blackburn	Hounslow
Rich city	Plymouth	Trafford
Poor city	Salford	Doncaster
Rich suburban	Bromsgrove	Chelmsford
Poor suburban	Ashfield	Blackpool
Rich rural	Mid Sussex	Kennet
Poor rural	Sedgemoor	Chichester

The intention was to carry out the survey in all 16 areas and to conduct the interviewing in one area from each pair. The areas for the interviewing were selected within each pair to reflect a geographical spread.

In addition, for the purposes of piloting the interviewing element of the research, an additional area of England was chosen. In view of the geographical spread of the 16 selected areas, Newcastle-upon-Tyne was chosen for this pilot. However, it was not included in the survey element of the research.

As will be explained later, it was subsequently decided also to undertake some additional data gathering in the Leeds–Bradford area.

Figure 2.1 *Areas in England from which the sample was taken.*

THE SAMPLE IN SCOTLAND, NORTHERN IRELAND AND WALES
With only three areas per country in the three other countries, it was not possible to replicate the sampling method used in England. In conjunction with the partner organisations in Scotland and Northern

Ireland (Aberlour Childcare Trust and the EXTERN Organisation respectively), it was decided to select the largest city in each country, one suburban area and one rural area, as it was felt that there might be considerable diversity in young people's experience in these different settings. Making use of census data, and taking into account the need for geographical spread, the suburban and rural areas were purposively selected.

This sampling method means that we cannot draw such precise estimates of the incidence of running away in the three countries. However, by making comparisons between similar areas in the different countries and with the larger English sample, it is possible to make a reasonably accurate estimate.

The sample areas selected in Wales, Scotland and Northern Ireland are shown in Table 2.2 and Figures 2.2 to 2.4.

Table 2.2 *Areas from which the sample in Scotland, Wales and Northern Ireland was taken*

Type of area	Scotland	Northern Ireland	Wales
City	Glasgow	Belfast	Cardiff
Suburban	Dunfermline	Carrickfergus	Merthyr Tydfil
Rural	Moray	Strabane	Meirionydd

In addition, some piloting of the survey method was carried out in South Wales, including at schools in Cardiff, Merthyr and Barry.

THE SURVEY

The aim of the survey was to gather information from a representative sample of young people under the age of 16. Because the likelihood of having run away increases with age, the oldest possible age group was selected in order to maximise the information. Given that the survey was carried out towards the end of the school year, it would not have been possible to cover a representative sample of young people aged 15 to 16 due to examination schedules and subsequent school leavers. Therefore, the survey was undertaken with 14- and 15-year-olds.

Figure 2.2 *Areas in Scotland from which the sample was taken.*

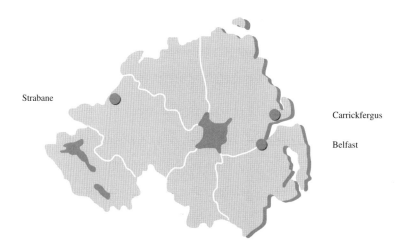

Figure 2.3 *Areas in Northern Ireland from which the sample was taken.*

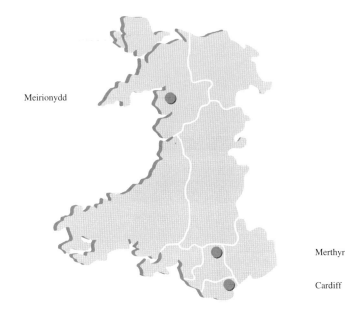

Meirionydd

Merthyr

Cardiff

Figure 2.4 *Areas in Wales from which the sample was taken.*

ACCESS

The main means of access to young people for the survey was through secondary schools. Initially, the directors of education were contacted in each area to seek approval for the research and permission to approach schools. Approval was granted in all 25 areas. A random sample of schools within each area was then chosen to select between 500 and 1,000 young people. In most cases, the sampling method used was simple random sampling, but in a few areas which had selective schools or a significant number of single-sex schools, the schools were chosen randomly from two or more groups.

These schools were then approached for consent to carry out the survey. If a school refused, which happened in about 10% of cases, a replacement school was chosen randomly and approached.

A weakness of seeking a representative sample of young people through secondary schools is that it tends to under-represent certain groups – in particular, young people who are regular non-attenders or are excluded from school, and young people with special needs. To compensate for this, additional surveys were carried out through pupil referral units and special schools in 50% of the areas.

PILOTING

A pilot of the whole survey process, from approaching directors of education through to analysing the data, was carried out in South Wales in January 1999 with around 1,000 young people in ten schools (eight mainstream, one private and one special needs). The pilot questionnaire included an additional section seeking young people's views on the questionnaire content. This provided valuable feedback, which resulted in modifications to the final questionnaire. Feedback was also gathered from the link teacher in each school.

The resulting modified questionnaire was then piloted in a school in Leeds in February 1999 and some further minor adjustments were made after this process.

METHODS

The procedure for administering the survey was usually for a person to visit the school to do a brief presentation to the year group about the research. This was followed by the distribution of questionnaires, either in assemblies or in Personal and Social Education lessons. Supply teachers were employed in each area on a sessional basis to undertake this task and were briefed by a member of the research team.

CONTENT

The questionnaire consisted of three sections. The first section, which was intended to be completed by all young people, gathered information about demographic characteristics, family forms or substitute care arrangements, quality of relationship with carers, school experiences, and personal issues. The second section asked specific questions about any experience the young person had of running away. The third section, again to be completed by all young people, asked for views and ideas about how young people who ran away, or were at risk of running away, could be helped. Some questions were in tick-box format, with room for additional comments where appropriate, whilst others were open-ended.

The intention of this content was threefold:

- to gather descriptive information about experiences of being away;

- to be able to explore links between running away and the key spheres of young people's lives – home, school and personal – aiming to build on research carried out in the USA (Brennan *et al.*, 1978) which found significant links in all these areas;

- to give young people the opportunity to be involved in the process of formulating responses to the issue of young people running away.

ETHICS

Careful consideration was given to the ethical issues involved in carrying out a survey into sensitive areas of young people's lives. The aim was to give young people control of the information that they contributed. The following ethical principles were agreed for the survey:

- Information would be provided to young people about the purposes of the research, and the ways in which it would be used, before they were asked to participate.

- The rights of young people to choose not to participate in the research would be emphasised and respected at all times.

- In view of the age of the young people taking part in the survey, it was decided that parental consent would not be sought for young people's participation. (However, it was necessary to seek parental consent in a few schools at the request of the local education authority concerned.)

- The survey would be anonymous, and no information given by young people would be passed on to anyone outside the research team, except within reports about the research findings.

- It was also agreed that individual schools would not be identified in any way.

OUTCOMES

The survey considerably exceeded the target of 5,000 young people. In total, almost 13,000 young people were surveyed in 113 mainstream secondary schools, six selective schools, six special needs schools, and nine pupil referral units. Unfortunately the questionnaires from one school arrived after the deadline for returns and it was not possible to include these in the analysis.

The overall proportion of young people in the schools who took part in the survey was over 80%. The main reason for non-participation was young people not being present when the survey was administered. The rate of refusal to participate was very low and, even including question-naires which were defaced or not filled in seriously, was less than 1%.

Inevitably, there was some variation in the numbers of young people surveyed by area. In three areas, it was not possible to reach the mini-mum target of 500 young people (due to the relatively small size of the school population in these areas and some schools declining to partici-pate). This was taken into account in the data analysis, making use of weighting where appropriate.

DATA PROCESSING AND ANALYSIS

The data from the questionnaires was put onto a database. Quantitative data was then transferred to SPSS (Statistical Products and Service Solutions) for statistical analysis, and the answers to open-ended ques-tions were transferred to TextSmart for initial analysis and coding.

The statistical analysis made use of a variety of robust non-paramet-ric tests. Chi-square tests were used for bivariate nominal data. Mann-Whitney and Kruskal-Wallis tests were used for bivariate data with one ordinal and one nominal variable. Correlations using Kendall's tau-b statistics were calculated for bivariate data involving two ordinal variables. Some multivariate analysis was carried out using logistic regression analysis and log-linear modelling.

Where a result is reported as statistically significant, this means that the p-value of the test was less than 0.01 (i.e. often termed '99% confi-dence') unless otherwise stated.

INTERVIEWS WITH PROFESSIONALS

Professionals interviewed included social workers, police officers, probation officers, youth workers, statutory and non-statutory sector housing workers, advice centre workers, and a variety of workers in other agencies.

There were several purposes in interviewing professionals:

• to gather their views;

• to identify other professionals that might be approached;

• to prepare the ground for visiting the area to interview young people.

METHODS

An initial list of people to contact was drawn up from a range of sources, including telephone directories and the internet. People were contacted by telephone and asked to do a short interview, which usually took less than 15 minutes. At the end of the interview, they were asked if they felt there were other professionals in the local area who might have knowledge relevant to the research, and also whether they or their agency would be willing to contribute further to the research. Any additional contacts were added to the list. This process continued until it seemed that no new names were being put forward.

At this stage, a small number of people were selected to be approached a second time for a more in-depth interview. These people were selected on the basis of their having a lot of relevant knowledge, and also in order that there were some perspectives on under-16s and some on 16- to 17-year olds from both statutory and non-statutory sectors. The second telephone interview was tape-recorded, with the consent of the research participant.

In addition, during both stages of the telephone interviewing, any relevant local research reports were identified and obtained where possible.

CONTENT

The content of the short interview was limited. The focus was on any knowledge the interviewee had of young people running away in the area, the numbers involved and the context in which this happened, plus information on what their agency did, and any other local information.

The longer interview went into more detail about the numbers and characteristics of young people who ran away in the area, the reasons for and contexts in which they ran away, what happened while they were away, and what gaps in services there were for this group of young people in the area.

ETHICS

Professionals being interviewed were guaranteed confidentiality (excluding very exceptional circumstances) and anonymity. Information on the research was posted to them in advance, and their consent to the interview being tape-recorded was obtained.

OUTCOMES

In total, over 500 professionals were contacted in 14 areas. Short interviews were carried out with over 350 professionals and over 100 of these people also contributed to the research through a longer interview.

DATA PROCESSING AND ANALYSIS

Information from both the long and short interviews, plus any local reports which were obtained, was placed on a database that was used for a thematic analysis of the interview content.

INTERVIEWS WITH YOUNG PEOPLE

ACCESS

In most cases, access to interview young people was arranged through the agencies contacted by telephone. Potentially suitable agencies were identified and recontacted by telephone. A date was then arranged for the visit and written materials were sent to the agency, including leaflets about the research to hand out to young people who might fit the research target group. The agencies that participated in the research in this way included youth advice and drop-in projects, youth and community centres, hostels, street-work projects and children's homes.

One or two interviewers would then visit the agency, discuss the research with young people who were interested in participating, and interview them if appropriate. Young people were paid £5 for their participation in the research. This payment was made before the interview started and was not dependent on the content of the interview or the length of time it took.

METHODS AND CONTENT

The interview process consisted of three phases. The first phase involved giving young people information about the research and the implications of their participation. This included explaining the ethical principles of the interviewing and in particular the policy on confidentiality. Young people had the opportunity to withdraw from the research after this first phase.

The second phase of the process involved a semi-structured interview covering a number of areas, including the young person's current situation, an overview of their life, detailed discussion about any times when they had run away, details about their involvement with school, social services and any other key agencies, and their views on what should be done to help young people who run away.

The third phase of the process involved a debriefing of the young person, checking out how they were feeling, returning to any issues arising out of the interview which the researcher was concerned about (e.g. child protection issues) and providing young people with information about local services where this might be helpful to them.

The interview was tape-recorded if the young person consented.

Following the interview, the interviewer wrote up notes from the interview in a standardised format.

ETHICS

The key ethical principles agreed for interviews with young people were as follows:

- Young people would be given as much information as was practical about the research aims and methods and how the findings would be used, in order that they could make an informed decision about whether to participate.

- Young people would be guaranteed confidentiality within certain limits. The limits were that, if any information was received which suggested that a person's life was in danger or that a person under 18 was at risk of serious harm, then confidentiality might have to be breached. If this were the case, it would happen with the young person's knowledge.

- Young people would be guaranteed anonymity and this meant that no case-study material would be used which could lead to the identification of an individual.

OUTCOMES

The process of engaging young people in the research was more successful than anticipated, and just over 200 interviews were carried out in 15 areas of the UK.

The interview sample consisted of a roughly equal split between females (48%) and males (52%).

Around half of the young people (48%) were aged 16 or 17, 10% were under 16, and 42% were aged 18 and over.

Using young people's own definitions, 12 young people were of black/African/Caribbean origin, five were of Asian origin, and eight were of mixed origin. This means that around 12% of the sample fell into one of these three categories. In the case of Asian young people, the information from individual interviews was supplemented by five group discussions carried out in Salford, Bradford and Leeds.

DATA PROCESSING AND ANALYSIS

As with the interviews with professionals, summarised information and quotes from the interviews were placed on a database which was used as a tool for analysis. Some analysis of every interview was carried out, including drawing up a pen picture of the young person's story, categorising issues experienced by the young person, and looking at their views about what services should be set up. However, we also wished to undertake a much more in-depth chronological analysis of young people's experiences, including the background context to running away, and a detailed breakdown of distinct phases of running away for each young person. In order to do this analysis, we selected a purposive sample of interviews balanced in terms of age of the first incident of running away, and type of area. This sample included 69 interviews. Of the 69 young people, 52 were under 16, and 17 were aged 16 to 17. In addition, we analysed all of the interviews with black young people in order to identify similarities and differences between young people of different origins.

PART 2

*Running away
or being forced
to leave under
the age of 16*

CHAPTER 3

Numbers and characteristics of young people who run away under the age of 16

In this chapter, we attempt to answer the question of how many young people under the age of 16 run away or are forced to leave home. There are considerable difficulties in attempting to estimate a phenomenon of this kind, which may be short-lived and hidden. We were able to overcome many of these potential difficulties by the survey method chosen. The survey was retrospective, thus capturing experiences over a period of time; it gathered information directly from young people and therefore overcame some of the difficulties involved in quantifying a hidden population; and it accessed a large-scale representative sample designed to smooth out local variations. We have therefore been able to arrive at good estimates of the scale and prevalence of being away from home amongst this age group, both overall and for various sub-groupings, which we present below. This is the first research which has been able authoritatively to make such estimates and to cover all four countries of the UK.

PREVALENCE ESTIMATES

As stated in Chapter 1, for the purposes of the research we have defined 'running away' as relating to young people under the age of 16 who either spend time away from home without parental permission, or are forced to leave home by their parents.

Overall, 16.5% of the young people surveyed had run away or been forced to leave at least once. Around three-fifths of these young people spent at least one night away from home on one of the occasions when they left – amounting to 10% of the young people surveyed.

However, these figures are likely to be under-estimates for two reasons. First, the fact that the survey was carried out in mainstream secondary schools means that young people who regularly do not attend school or who are excluded will be under-represented. We gathered additional information from a sample of such young people and, as will be discussed later, in Chapter 6, their running-away rate was much higher than average. Second, we surveyed young people aged 14 to 15. At the time when the survey was carried out, the ages of these young people was between 14 years, 4 months and 15 years, 9 months, with a median age of around 15 years, 1 month. As we will see later in this chapter, not surprisingly, the likelihood of running away increases steadily with age. Thus, the above figures will be under-estimates because many young people will run away for the first time after the survey but before their sixteenth birthday.

The 15-year-olds (with an estimated median age of 15 years, 5 months) in the survey were significantly more likely (10.4%) to have run away than the 14-year-olds (8.7%) (with an estimated median age of 14 years, 9 months). It is possible to project from this that, by their sixteenth birthday, around 11% of the sample would have run away. We would therefore estimate that at least one in nine young people run away overnight one or more times before the age of 16. On the basis of this projection it is estimated that around 77,000 young people under 16 run away for the first time each year.

These estimates are projections taking into account the factors discussed above. However, throughout the rest of the report the running away rates quoted for various groups are those occurring in the survey sample.

The main survey also did not adequately cover young people with special needs, and we will present some findings from a supplementary sample of these young people later. However, the fact that only a small minority of the population of young people attend special needs schools means that this gap in the main sample will not affect the overall estimates.

PREVALENCE ESTIMATES FOR INDIVIDUAL COUNTRIES

We have already described the sampling strategy in Chapter 2. Given the much larger population of England, we sampled 16 areas, using stratified random sampling and are able to arrive at fairly accurate estimates of the prevalence of running away. In the other three countries, we were able to sample only three areas, and thus the estimates for these countries are less conclusive.

The prevalence estimates for each country are shown in Table 3.1.

Table 3.1 *Prevalence estimates of young people running away in England, Northern Ireland, Scotland and Wales*

Country	Number of young people surveyed	% running away overnight
England	8164	10%
Northern Ireland	1310	9%
Scotland	1802	10%
Wales	1214	8.5%

As can be seen in the table, there is some variation in prevalence rates between the countries. However, statistical tests suggest that these differences are not large enough to be significant. Our evidence suggests, therefore, that there is no evidence of a significant difference in rates of running away between the four countries.

VARIATIONS IN RUNNING AWAY BETWEEN AREAS

A central aim of the research was to fill the gap in knowledge about the experiences of young people who do not live in large cities and conurbations. The sampling strategy was designed with this aim in mind. We ensured that the survey was carried out in a range of areas according to population density and economic prosperity.

The most reliable estimates we have here are for England, due to the size of the sample. Twelve of the 16 areas were selected specifically on the basis of population density (city, suburban and rural) and economic prosperity.

A comparison of areas according to population density is shown in Table 3.2.

Table 3.2 *Percentage of runaways according to population density of area*

Type of area	Number of young people surveyed	% running away overnight
City (excluding London)	3049	11%
Suburban	2291	10%
Rural	1275	10%

Again, there are small variations here, with the rates looking a little higher in city areas, but these are not statistically significant.

Comparisons of the three types of areas in Scotland, Northern Ireland and Wales also show no evidence of a difference in running-away rates.

Amongst the English sample, we surveyed three London areas (not included in the above 'city' category). Interestingly, comparing these areas with the categories in Table 3.2, we found that the running away rates were significantly lower in London than elsewhere both in terms of running away overall and running away overnight (7.5%). This finding is not conclusive because we did not specifically select a sample which is representative of London as a whole. However, it seems highly unlikely that running-away rates in London are higher than anywhere else in the UK.

We are also able to make some comparisons between the above 12 England areas on the basis of economic prosperity. We found that running-away rates were marginally higher in less prosperous areas, but again this difference was not statistically significant. We discuss this issue further in Chapter 6, Structural Context.

RATES OF RUNNING AWAY FOR DIFFERENT GROUPS

As previous research has indicated, the rates of running away are not uniform amongst all groups of young people. Here, we look at variations in rates according to gender, ethnicity and age. Variations in rate according to other factors, e.g. different family forms, or experience of substitute care, are dealt with in Chapters 5 and 6. In this section, and throughout the rest of the report, all statistics relate to running away or being forced to leave home over night, unless we explicitly state otherwise.

GENDER

As with previous research, e.g. Rees (1993), the survey indicates that females (11.5%) are more likely to experience at least one incident of being away than males (8.5%). However, as we will see below and later in the report, there are other notable differences in patterns of being away between the sexes which show a more complex picture.

ETHNICITY

Previous research by Abrahams and Mungall (1992) and Rees (1993) found significantly higher rates of running away amongst African-Caribbean young people than amongst white young people, and significantly lower rates of running away amongst young people of Indian/Pakistani/Bangladeshi origin.

However, the current survey shows a different picture. The rates of being away overnight are highest amongst white young people (10.5%), followed by young people of African-Caribbean origin (7.5%) and then young people of Indian/Pakistani/ Bangladeshi origin (around 5.5%). This variation between young people of different origins was statistically significant.

These findings warrant a slightly more detailed presentation of the data. Looking first at the young people of African-Caribbean origin, not only were the national figures comparable to those of white young people but, in addition, those in the two areas selected for the sample with a particularly high proportion of young people of this origin (Lambeth and Hackney) were fairly close to those for white young people.

For young people of Indian/Pakistani/Bangladeshi origin, the picture is more mixed. In London, the rate of being away amongst this group (4.5%) is lower than for white young people (8.5%), but not significantly so. However, in Blackburn, the difference is significant, with only 3% of young people of Indian/Pakistani/Bangladeshi origin having been away, compared to 12% of white young people in the area.

The above analysis suggests that there may be a difference between London and other areas here. It seems possible that running away rates are more similar for young people of different ethnic groups in London than outside London.

Nevertheless, the rates of being away amongst Asian young people appear to be higher than previously thought, even outside London.

AGE AT WHICH YOUNG PEOPLE FIRST RAN AWAY

Around a quarter of the young people had first run away or been forced to leave before the age of 11.

Males had first run away at a younger age than females. Thirty per cent of males had first run away under the age of 11 compared to 19% of the females. There were more than twice as many females as males in the group who had first run away from the age of 14 upwards.

There were no significant differences in the age of first running away for young people from different ethnic groups, or for young people living in different types of areas.

NUMBER OF TIMES YOUNG PEOPLE RUN AWAY

Over half (54%) of the young people who had run away had done so once and a further quarter had run away twice. Around one in eight (12%) had run away more than three times.

Looking only at those who had run away overnight, the proportion of repeat (more than three times) incidence is higher (around 15%). On the basis of these findings we project that there are around 129,000 incidents of young people running away over night each year in the UK.

As one might expect, there was a significant correlation between age of first running away and number of times away. Young people who had started running away at a younger age tended to have run away more often. More than half (53%) of the young people who had run away more than three times had first run away before the age of 11. (Some caution is needed here because the survey was carried out with 14- to 15-year-olds and so some of the young people who had recently started to run away may run away on further occasions after the survey was administered. This would mean that the 53% figure above might be a slight over-estimate.)

This is an important finding as it suggests the need for some preventative interventions to be aimed at young people before they reach secondary school. Forty-five per cent of those young people who had first run away before the age of eight, and a quarter (27%) of those who had first run away between the ages of eight and ten went on to run away more than three times. These figures compare with only 9% of those who had first run away from the age of 11 onwards.

Males had run away more times on average than females. Thus, there were more females than males amongst those who had run away one to three times, but more males than females who had run away more than three times. Nineteen per cent of males were in this latter group compared to 12% of females.

There were no significant differences in the number of times that young people in different ethnic groups had run away.

There were no significant differences by type of area (rural, suburban, city).

Ran away or forced to leave?

The large majority of young people classified themselves as having run away, but almost a fifth (19%) of those who had run away overnight said that they had been forced to leave home.

There were no differences between males and females in this respect.

There was a marginally significant difference between young people of different ethnic groups regarding being forced to leave. Young people of African-Caribbean origin and Indian/Pakistani/Bangladeshi origin were more likely to be forced to leave than young people of white origin. However, there is a slightly more significant difference between type of area and being forced to leave. Those young people living in London were significantly more likely to have been forced to leave, or less likely to have run away than young people outside London. A three-way analysis of ethnicity, area and running away/being forced to leave suggests that it is living in London which is the significant factor here, rather than ethnicity.

This piece of information must be considered in conjunction with the difference in overall rates of running away between areas, as described above. Young people in London were less likely to run away than young people in other areas. In fact, the rates of being forced to leave home overnight are almost identical in all four types of areas. What we can conclude from this, then, is not that young people in London are more likely to be forced to leave home but that they are significantly less likely to run away or choose to leave home.

Looking at the overall picture, we would estimate that around one in fifty young people are forced to leave home and are away overnight before the age of 16. This amounts to around 14,000 young people in each school year cohort.

SUMMARY

We have presented the evidence on the prevalence of running away both overall and for the different countries and different types of areas which make up the UK. Overall, we estimate that 11% of young people run away for one night or more on one or more occasions before the age of 16, amounting to around 77,000 young people running away for the first time each year. This prevalence rate is remarkably stable across the different countries and also between different types of areas, categorised by population density and economic prosperity. At first glance, these findings may seem rather bland. However, they are of considerable importance in that they represent, for the first time, firm and reliable evidence that there is a significant prevalence of running away in all parts of the UK. The implication of this is clearly that services must be developed in all kinds of areas and in all four countries if there is to be an effective and inclusive response to the needs of young people who run away. Whilst many young people only run away once, others go on to run away repeatedly. We estimate that there are a total of around 129,000 incidents of running away over night per year in the UK.

There are differences in running away for different groups. The likelihood of running away increases with age, and females are more likely to run away than males. There are also differences according to ethnicity, with some evidence that young people of Indian/Pakistani/Bangladeshi origin are somewhat less likely to run away. However, the rates of running away across different ethnic groups are much more similar than previous research has suggested.

The survey also illustrated a significant prevalence of young people feeling that they are forced to leave home. Almost a fifth of young people who had 'run away' classified themselves as having been forced to leave home. We estimate that around 14,000 young people in each school year cohort are forced to leave home before the age of 16.

CHAPTER 4

Why young people run away

Earlier research (Rees, 1993; Wade *et al.*, 1998) made the distinction between two ways of answering the question of why young people run away: triggers and contexts. Triggers for running away are the reasons for making the decision to run away on a specific occasion. Contexts refer to the background and historical factors which contributed to the situation in which running away took place. Whilst triggers and contexts may to a certain extent be the same, e.g. being hit as a trigger and a history of physical abuse as a context, it is often the case that there may be a wide range of contextual factors whilst there is a quite specific trigger. For this reason, the distinction between triggers and context seems to be a helpful one and we will employ it in this report. In this chapter, we will focus on triggers for running away or being forced to leave. The two following chapters, Chapters 5 and 6, will consider context.

We will only consider information from the survey in this chapter; information on triggers from the interviews will be incorporated later in the report (Chapter 8). As the current research is the first in the UK to have gathered information on reasons for running away from a large representative sample of young people, the findings in this chapter are of considerable significance in developing an understanding of why young people run away.

We do not consider evidence from the survey on triggers for running away from substitute care because our sample of these young people is relatively small and a recent research report (Wade *et al.*, 1998) provides much more reliable information than we could offer on this issue.

In the survey questionnaire, young people were asked two questions about triggers for running away. First, they were asked an open-ended question about why they had run away. Second, they were asked to select from a list of general descriptions for running away: problems at home, problems at school, personal problems, and other reasons.

Looking at the second question first, young people's responses are shown in Table 4.1. It should be noted that some young people selected more than one option.

Table 4.1 *Broad reasons for running away from home*

Problems at home	80%
Personal problems	35%
Problems at school	23%
Other reasons	13%

The responses substantiated the view that it is primarily issues within the family which lead to young people running away. Four-fifths of the young people identified problems within the family as one of the reasons for running away. For the 20% of young people who did not identify a family problem, around half (48%) had a personal problem, over a third (38%) indicated 'other reasons', and a quarter (25%) had problems at school. (Again more than one response was given in some cases here.)

We will now go on to consider each of these four areas in order of prevalence.

PROBLEMS AT HOME

In order to look systematically at the various problems at home that can trigger running away, it was necessary to categorise the open-ended responses that young people gave. Some responses were quite general whilst others focused on one specific issue or a number of related issues, e.g. arguments and being hit. Any categorisation of these responses necessarily implies a level of interpretation and we have provided numerous quotes in order to give some indication of the kinds of responses which led to each categorisation.

For just over a quarter of the sample (27%), it was not possible to identify any specific issue, but there were general problems at home, often including arguments.

For the remainder of young people who were having problems at home, it was possible to identify at least one issue that triggered the most recent running away incident. We will deal with these issues in order of their incidence, discussing all reasons mentioned by at least 1% of the young people.

PHYSICAL VIOLENCE OR THREAT OF VIOLENCE

This was the most common specific reason for running away, mentioned by 12% of young people. We include in this category young people who either reported being physically hit by a parent (10%) or reported fearing that this would happen (2%).

We are not able to generalise about the level of physical abuse that this entails, but it is clear that for some of the young people this was repeated and/or ongoing:

> [I ran away] *because my father beat me with a bat because I dropped my mum's photo and it smashed. He bruised my whole body and cut my face.*

> *I was sick of being used as punch bag.*

> *I ran away because my mum kept shouting at me, she got drunk and strangled me.*

In some cases, this was linked to domestic violence:

> *I caught my mum and dad arguing. My dad hit my mum and I went and tried to talk to him but he hit me instead.*

Mothers and fathers were mentioned equally often as abusers. This is a difficult finding to interpret as mothers tend to spend more time with their children and also single parents are more likely to be women. However, the idea that physical abuse by mothers as well as fathers is commonplace is consistent with a review of findings from the USA on adolescent abuse (Rees and Stein, 1999, forthcoming).

EMOTIONAL ABUSE

Definitions of emotional abuse are difficult to draw up. Here, we include young people who reported being scapegoated or regularly maligned by their parents and those who were treated differently to siblings. In all, 9% of young people (excluding those who had been physically abused) mentioned one of these factors, with the large majority mentioning scapegoating:

> [I ran away] *because I had a problem in my family and I was the one who would always get blamed for something that I never did.*

In some cases, there was evidence of other forms of systematic abuse:

> *I was being shouted at and my father kept breaking my things. He threw my Walkman at the wall and it broke.*

EMOTIONAL NEGLECT

Here, we include feelings of rejection and neglect by family that have not already been covered in the above categories. This category accounted for 6% of the young people, many of whom felt unloved in their families:

> *I ran away because my mum, dad and brother they all hated me and I thought I outstayed my welcome and thought they didn't want me no more.*

> *I felt unloved and unwanted.*

PARENTAL DISHARMONY

For young people in this category (6%), the main trigger was wanting to get away from conflict between their parents. Often, this conflict was related to the parents splitting up:

> *Because my parents divorced. The first time I ran away was because of this.*

In some cases, this had repercussions for the young person:

> *I ran away because my parents were splitting up and all the anger and blame was pointed at me.*

STEP-PARENT ISSUES

Some of the above categories, e.g. physical violence and emotional abuse, have included issues relating to step-parents as well as birth parents. As we will show in Chapter 5, issues relating to step-families are an important factor in understanding running away. Here, we consider triggers for young people which were connected with a poor relationship with a step-parent, but where there was no mention of abuse. This was the case for 4% of the young people who had run away overnight:

> 'Cause my step-dad did my head in and I was going through a bad stage.

> I ran away because we had just moved to a new area due to trouble with my step-dad. My mum started dating a new boyfriend and he moved in. I felt that he was intruding and that me and my brothers didn't want him there.

BOUNDARIES AND CONTROL

For a further 4% of the young people, the main trigger for running away was a disagreement with parents relating to boundaries, discipline and control. Sometimes, this was just a general unhappiness at being 'grounded', whilst in other cases the young person felt that they were not being treated appropriately for their age:

> Because I didn't like my dad because he is strict and he used to tell me to be in at 9 p.m. and my friends were out longer and I was grounded for dodging school.

PRESSURE FROM PARENTS

Around 3% of young people mentioned pressure from parents as the main trigger for running away, often linked to school issues:

> Because my family were pressuring me and it got too much for me. They made me tidy after them when I was in the middle of my exams and once I found out I had failed they got really mad at me and I'm not saying any more.

POOR QUALITY OF RELATIONSHIPS

A further 3% of young people cited poor quality relationships at home as the reason for running away. This included young people who did not feel trusted and those who did not feel listened to.

BEING IN TROUBLE WITH PARENTS

Some young people (3%) who cited problems at home ran away primarily because of being in trouble with the police, or with drugs or alcohol. We will discuss the role of these issues further later in this chapter.

PROBLEMS WITH SIBLINGS

Although relatively uncommon, problems with siblings were the primary factor for some young people (3%):

> *Because me and my brother was always fighting and he always put me down. I felt bad.*

PARENTAL PROBLEMS

Finally, 1% of young people said they ran away to get away from problems that their parents were having. In most cases, this was to do with a parent's alcohol use:

> *Because I couldn't handle my mum's drinking any more. I couldn't cope with the bullying.*

BEING FORCED TO LEAVE

We have used the term 'run away' for brevity in the above discussion, but in fact about a fifth of the young people who had been away over night said that they had been forced to leave home rather than running away. In some cases, this was an overt action on the part of parents:

> *I left because me and my mum don't get on. We always argue and she was really depressed and told me I had to go as I was making her unhappy.*

> *Because my step-father was hitting me and I told my dad and I told him about sexually abusing me and my mum found out and didn't believe me. Most of my family fell out with me and my mum decided she didn't want anything to do with me any more.*

In other cases, it seems to be more that the young person felt they had to leave for their own emotional or physical well-being:

> *My mum and step-dad went through a rough patch and got violent so I had to go and stay with my friends and then dad.*

We will go on to discuss some of the specific characteristics of this group of young people in Chapter 8.

PERSONAL PROBLEMS

After problems at home, personal problems were the next most common mentioned by young people in the survey.

Many of these young people were unwilling to give details of why they ran away:

No comment. My business.

or were unspecific:

I had just gone through a very bad experience in my life a couple of months beforehand and it all got too much trying to cope with it on my own. I couldn't tell anyone about it as it would only hurt them too much.

Others mentioned issues such as needing a break or problems at school that are discussed elsewhere.

The most common issues specifically mentioned are listed below.

DEPRESSION AND ANGER

Depression was mentioned as a reason for running away by 4% of those who had run away overnight, three-quarters of whom were female:

I was depressed, my family had split up and I felt lonely.

Anger management was only mentioned by two young people – one female, one male.

RELATIONSHIPS

Around 3% of the young people mentioned issues connected to relationships with boyfriends or girlfriends as a reason for running away. All but one of these young people were female and the issue was commonly that their parent(s) did not approve of their relationship and attempted to place boundaries on it which the young person resented:

My dad said I am not allowed out, I'm not allowed to see my boyfriend and I should finish with him.

With one exception, these young people said that they ran away rather than were forced to leave home.

PEER ISSUES

The reasons given by young people for running away include a variety of references to peers. Around 3.5% (mostly female) mentioned bullying by peers as a sole or contributory factor to running away:

> *I got fed up and was really upset about being bullied for being fat.*

In addition, a small number mentioned problems with friends as a factor.

A handful of young people (1%) said that they ran away to accompany a friend who was unhappy.

A few young people also mentioned 'getting in with the wrong crowd' as a factor in their conflict with parents which led to them running away.

Clearly, some of the above issues are only relevant for a small number of young people. However, around one in twelve of the young people who ran away mentioned one of the above peer or relationship issues as a reason for running away, so the influence of peer relationships on running away is not negligible.

TROUBLE WITH THE POLICE

Around 3% of young people (three-quarters male) mentioned this as a reason for running away overnight, either to avoid the police or due to parental reactions:

> *I had to leave one night because I'd got into trouble with the police and my dad didn't want me in the house until he had calmed down.*

ALCOHOL USE

Around 2% mentioned problems with or use of alcohol as one of the reasons that they ran away (fearing parents' reactions) or were forced to leave.

DRUGS USE

Only a small minority (around 1%) mentioned drugs use as a reason for running away or being forced to leave home.

PROBLEMS AT SCHOOL

Whilst nearly a quarter of young people indicated that problems at school had contributed to them running away from home, this was usually in conjunction with problems at home and specific school issues were often not mentioned in answer to the open-ended question about reasons for running away.

Problems related to truancy and parents' reactions (or feared reactions) to this were mentioned by about 2% of young people as a contributory factor to their running away:

> I missed school and got caught. My parents were telling me what an embarrassment I was and how they were ashamed of me so I thought it would be better if I left.

Other school-related problems were mentioned by slightly more young people (about 4%). Some of these problems were not explained by the young people, but specific comments included not wanting to go to school, feeling lonely at school, being shouted at by teachers, and being teased or bullied:

> I was scared because I kept having panic attacks because people were getting to me bullying, picking on me, calling me, and I was getting shouted at by my teachers and the headmaster.

There was also the issue of pressure from parents to achieve at school, covered earlier under problems at home, which accounted for around 3% of young people.

In all then, around 8% to 10% of young people mentioned specific school-related issues as contributing to their running away.

OTHER REASONS

Whilst 13% of young people ticked the 'Other reasons' box, many of these had also indicated that they had problems at home, personal problems or problems at school, and their reasons for running away have already been categorised. So, in fact, only 7% of young people ticked 'Other reasons' solely.

Half of these young people did not give a response to the open-ended question about reasons for running away so we have no further information on what led them to leave home. For those who did respond, three reasons predominated. These were: being in trouble, needing freedom, and needing a break. To some extent, the first and third categories have already been covered above. The distinctive cate-

gory is needing freedom. However, in total, those who run away to
have freedom or to have fun accounted for less than 1% of those who
had run away overnight.

SUMMARY

In this chapter, we have spent some time examining the reasons for
running away given by young people on the survey questionnaire. This
information is of considerable importance because it is the first reliable data on reasons for running away gathered from a representative
sample of young people.

The findings indicate that problems at home strongly predominate
amongst the reasons for young people running away. Four out of every
five young people cited these problems as one of the reasons why they
ran away, and it is clear from an analysis of young people's responses
that in most cases problems at home are the primary reason. This finding is hardly surprising but is important in conclusively disproving the
idea that young people commonly run away for fun or for trivial reasons.

Amongst those who run away due to problems at home, general
conflict appears to be the most common factor. However, the next
most common reasons are physical abuse, emotional abuse and
neglect, which together accounted for over a quarter (27%) of those
who ran away due to problems at home. The large number of other
family problems which can trigger running away indicate that running
away is potentially a response by the young person to a wide range of
difficulties in their lives.

Other reasons for running away are of much less significance, but
problems with peers and problems at school appear to be important
factors for a substantial minority of young people.

CHAPTER 5

The home context

In this first of two chapters on the context in which running away takes place, we consider factors related to the place the young person was living before running away. Previous UK and US research (Rees, 1993; Brennan *et al.*, 1978) has indicated that the home context is a primary influence on young people running away. In this chapter, we make use of the survey, the interviews with young people, and the interviews with professionals to look at some of the factors associated with running away and also at protective factors which militate against the likelihood of young people running away.

We will first consider the family context and later go on to consider substitute care. The term 'family' here relates to the household unit in which the young person lives. Where we refer to other family members, we will use the term 'extended family'. However, we need to be aware that the meaning and concept of the family differs in different cultural contexts.

THE FAMILY CONTEXT

We will first look at information from the survey about young people's family context and then go on to consider the information from the interviews with the professionals and young people.

INFORMATION FROM THE SURVEY

In the survey, we gathered information both about the family forms within which young people lived, and about young people's feelings about their parents or carers. This information relates to young people's situation at the time they filled in the questionnaire, which is not necessarily the same as their situation at the time they ran away.

However, it is useful in order to explore the broad relationship between family context and running away. When we consider the information from the interviews with young people later in this chapter, we will look more closely at the chronology of family events and how they interact with the incidence of running away.

Around seven in ten young people lived with both birth parents, two in ten with a lone parent, and one in ten with a parent and step-parent.

The rate of running away differed significantly for these three main family forms, as shown in Table 5.1.

Table 5.1 *Rates of running away according to different family forms*

Family form	% running away overnight
Two birth parents	7%
Lone parent	13%
Parent and step-parent	21%

The differences here are large. Looked at a different way, young people in step-parent households made up almost 20% of those who had run away, although they made up only 10% of the total sample of young people.

This finding mirrors earlier research (Rees, 1993). The Rees study suggested that the effect of economic disadvantage could explain some of the differences in rates of running away by family form. However, in the current survey, this is not the case. The differences in rates of running away by family form remain just as significant when economic factors are taken into account (see Chapter 6 for further discussion of this issue).

The clear link between family forms and running away leads to the question of what it is about these forms which is more or less likely to give rise to running away. We will look at this evidence shortly. Before we do so, we will look at young people's overall experience of living in families.

The quality of relationships with parents or carers
Brennan *et al.* (1978) in the USA found that running away was linked to a number of aspects of parent–child relationships. These conclusions were drawn from the employment of an extensive range of scales. We were not able to replicate this detailed data gathering, but included six questions concerning young people's relationships with their parents or carers:

1. Are your parent(s) too strict?

2. Do you get on well with your parent(s)?

3. Do your parent(s) treat you fairly compared to your brothers and sisters?

4. Do you feel your parent(s) understand you?

5. Do your parent(s) ever hit you?

6. Do you feel your parent(s) care about you?

Young people who did not live with a parent were asked to answer the questions about whichever adults they did live with.

In making use of this information, we are not suggesting that young people's responses represent the reality about their relationships with parents. Clearly, parents and other people may have very different perspectives to those of the young people.

Table 5.2 *Young people's views of relationships with parents: those who had run away compared with those who had not*

Survey question	% of young people who had not run away	% of young people who had run away
Parents too strict	7%	20%
Don't get on with parents	4%	20%
Don't feel treated fairly	12%	34%
Don't feel understood	8%	29%
Parents hit a lot	2%	10%
Don't feel cared about	2%	8%

Each of these questions proved a significant discriminator between young people who run away and those who do not. Table 5.2 shows the proportion of young people who had a negative view of relationships with parents on each of the six questions, broken down according to whether the young person had run away or not.

Not surprisingly, a combination of all six factors also proves a significant discriminator, as shown in Table 5.3.

Table 5.3 *Relation between the quality of family relationships and running away*

Quality of family relationships	% who had run away overnight
Good (0 negative responses)	6%
Moderate (1 to 2 negative responses)	16%
Poor (3 to 4 negative responses)	38%
Very poor (5 to 6 negative responses)	52%

Thus, over half of those who gave five or six negative responses to the list of items had run away, and over a third of those who gave three or four negative responses, had run away.

It is possible to analyse the relative importance of the above six items in terms of explaining running away. A combined analysis of the influence of all six items suggests that the items for parental strictness and not feeling cared about are not significant when considered in conjunction with the other four items.

The above analysis clearly indicates that there is a relationship between young people's feelings about relationships with their parent(s) or carer(s) and the likelihood of them having run away.

The link between family forms and quality of family relationships
Returning to the discussion on family forms, we looked at young people's feelings about relationships with parents for the different family forms. There were significant differences for five of the six items used on the questionnaire.

For four of these items (getting on with parents, feeling treated fairly, feeling understood and feeling cared about) young people living with both birth parents expressed the most positive feelings, followed by young people living with a lone parent, and then young people living with a parent and step-parent. In terms of parental strictness, young people living with a parent and step-parent were more likely to feel that their parents were too strict, compared with the other two family forms which were roughly equal on this item. The only item which did not show a significant difference by family form was young people being hit.

So, given these differences, can the different rates of running away amongst the different family forms be explained by young people's responses to the six questions about relationships with parents? The answer to this question is a qualified 'no'. An initial combined analysis of the influence of family form and the six relationship items suggests that both have a discernible influence on running away. That is to say that, even looking at young people who have similar feelings about their relationships with their parents, young people living in step- or lone-parent families are still more likely to run away than young people living with both birth parents. For example, the overall running-away rate amongst young people who felt that they got on poorly with their parent(s) or carer(s) was 36%. However, this varied according to family form, being 28% for young people who lived with both birth parents, 39% for those who lived with a lone parent, and 48% for those who lived with a parent and step-parent.

The above findings suggest that, whilst disharmony in the relationship between young people and parents is a significant factor influencing running away, young people in lone-parent and step-parent families are more likely to run away when disharmony does occur. However, more detailed analysis suggests that, for the minority of young people who responded negatively to most of the family relationship items, tests failed to show a statistically significant difference in running-away rates for young people living in different family forms.

In summary then, where there is little or moderate disharmony, young people living with both birth parents are less likely to run away than young people living in other family forms. That is, where a young person is dissatisfied primarily about one aspect of family relationships (e.g. being treated differently to siblings) young people living with a single parent or in a step-family are more likely to run away than young people living with both birth parents. However, where there is more serious disharmony, that is where young people are dis-satisfied about a number of aspects of relationships with parents, there is probably little or no difference between young people's likelihood of running away in different family forms.

INFORMATION FROM THE INTERVIEWS WITH PROFESSIONALS

We now turn to the interviewing of professionals to explore their perspectives on the above issues.

It is notable that less than half (48%) of the professionals inter-viewed for the research came into contact with young people under the age of 16 running away, compared to almost all (93%) in relation to the 16- to 17-year-old age group. Consequently, the comments on the context in which this happens are more limited than those we will con-sider later for the over-16 age group.

In terms of family context, professionals identified two key overlap-ping areas – issues arising out of family forms and changes to family forms, and issues regarding the quality of relationships between young people and their parents. So there was a view that, whilst for many young people it was specific aspects of their relationships with parents which formed the background context to their running away, for other young people it was also the simple fact of the disruption of changing family forms which was important.

In the second context, professionals mentioned the effect of parental separation and divorce, general issues of family breakdown, and the introduction of step-parents as contributing factors in themselves, irre-spective of the quality of family relationships. For example:

People not knowing how to approach their new step-mother or step-father or the new step-mother or new step-father not knowing how to approach the other children. We come across that one a lot.

In the first context, they cited physical, sexual and emotional abuse, neglect, rejection, arguments and conflict as important contextual fac-tors for young people running away. These issues were often of a long-standing nature:

By the time we see them at 12 or 13, they've had a huge amount of history there that we never get close to understanding.

In connection with this general pattern of conflictual and abusive relationships, a number of workers pointed to a lack of parenting skills in managing and resolving conflict:

> *The way that they resolve a dispute ... is usually a shout, a scream, a violent argument and very often a thump.*

These views seem to concur with the findings from the survey in the sense that poor relationships between young people and parents make running away more likely irrespective of family form, but there are additional stresses of living in families where changes in form have taken place which also make running away more likely.

In addition to these two key areas, two other themes came over from the interviews with professionals. First, for a minority of young people, there was a feeling that parents were unable to cope with their behaviour. This included young people with 'uncontrollable' behaviour as well as those who had problems with drugs or alcohol. The tensions created by these issues could lead to young people running away or being forced to leave:

> *They can't cope with what their children are getting involved with and that basically they have no control, that they're truanting from school and all the other things that go with that.*

Second, some professionals identified parents' drug or alcohol problems as a contextual factor in the lives of some young people who run away:

> *Young people leave home if their parent(s) drink heavily because they do not want to stay at home because of the risk of violence and the emotional distress of the situation.*

INFORMATION FROM THE INTERVIEWS WITH YOUNG PEOPLE

The interviews with young people gave us the opportunity to explore some of the above issues in more detail. One of the strengths of the interview data is that we were usually able to establish a chronology of family events, which provides information not available in the survey data. We will focus first in this section on young people's accounts of their family context before running away began; then we will go on to look at the developing family context for those who run away repeatedly.

The family context before running away

We divided the young people who had run away under the age of 16 into two groups on the basis of whether they had first run away before the age of 11. This enabled us to examine whether there were differences amongst the two groups and to draw out any key messages for the younger age group. This seemed important, as the survey identified that a substantial proportion of young people who start running away before secondary school age subsequently run away more than three times.

A comparison of the two groups suggests that, whilst they had quite a lot in common, there were some interesting differences. The issues experienced by young people in both groups fall into three broad areas – changes in family form, parenting, and parental problems.

The majority of young people had experienced a change in family form due to parents separating or divorcing, bereavement or being moved into care. Additionally, in around a third of the families, a step-parent had been introduced at some point before the young person started running away. A comparison by age of first running away suggests that those young people who had run away younger were more likely to have experienced one or more of the above events before running away, even though there would have been less time in which this could happen.

Parenting issues were important contextual factors for more than half the young people. Physical abuse was the most common of these issues, but there were also a number of young people who had experienced each of the following: sexual abuse, emotional abuse, neglect and rejection. We use the term 'physical abuse' where young people's accounts suggest that this was usually of a serious and/or repetitive nature:

My daddy used to abuse me physically. I've been to hospital loads of times, bruised ribs, black eyes, broken wrists and arms.

Mum used to slap my head really hard, punch me whilst sitting on me; her various men also did it. One of them pushed me on the nettles, another pushed me against the window.

Where the issue of sexual abuse was part of the family context, the emotional and relationship issues raised by the abuse were often as significant as the abuse itself:

When I was about 11, my dad used to sexually abuse me but I didn't want to upset my mum. Basically, I knew that if my mum and dad split up, my dad would have gone to prision and my brother would have had nowhere to live, he would have ended up in care. It was a bit scary. I didn't tell my mum; my brother knows but I haven't told anybody else. It's really hard to know what to do.

In some cases, the experience of being sexually abused was exacerbated by the reactions of others when the young person disclosed the abuse. Some of the young people interviewed encountered disbelief and rejection by the other parent (usually female) when they did disclose the abuse.

In addition, a number of young people interviewed perceived differential treatment of siblings as an important issue for them before they started running away. In all of these cases, the young person felt less favoured than her/his siblings.

Again, there were indications of differences between the two age groups here, with a suggestion that young people who first ran away before the age of 11 were more likely to have experienced abuse prior to running away. Again, it is notable that there would have been less time in which this could have taken place for these young people.

The third broad area of family context was problems which parents themselves were experiencing. Around a third of the young people lived in families with one or more of the following issues: domestic violence by a male partner towards a female partner, parental alcohol problems, parental drug addiction, and parental mental health problems. These issues seemed to be more prevalent before running away for the older age group, although of course it may be that those young people who ran away younger were less aware of these issues before they ran away.

In general then, there are some indications that the family contexts of young people who run away before the age of 11 are more disrupted and abusive than for young people who start to run away at older ages.

An additional issue which was not present for those young people who first ran away before the age of 11 related to young people's behaviours and parental reactions to these. A few of the young people were violent towards other family members, and some spoke of arguments with parents stemming from their (the young person's) use of alcohol or drugs. This echoes the professionals' views about parents having difficulty in coping with young people's behaviour.

The developing family context
We will now briefly consider the developing family context for those young people in the interview sample who ran away repeatedly.

To a great extent, these issues were the same as before young people started running away. Only three of the young people started to experience physical abuse after they first ran away. Given the high incidence of physical abuse before running away began, this is a notable finding. There were some new instances of bereavement, conflict, issues around boundaries, family breakdown, and geographical instability after running away had begun, although there is nothing particular to note in these cases. It seems that in the majority of cases these issues are present before young people start running away, if they are going to be present at all. Similarly, differential treatment of siblings and parental problems were not mentioned as fresh issues by young people after they started running away.

Thus, our analysis suggests that most of the problematic issues in the family context that form the backdrop to young people running away are present before running away starts. Relatively few additional problems arise at a later point.

Only one new issue was identified in the family context of young people after running away began. Four young people mentioned making contact with an absent parent. These young people were all disappointed with the outcomes of their contact:

> When I was 15, my natural mother rang me. We met... [I] met my natural dad and brother and sister. Things went bad.

One young person had turned to his father when he was forced to leave by his mother and had been rejected:

> My dad didn't really want anything to do with me at the time and I didn't really want anything to do with him.

Issues relating specifically to African-Caribbean and Asian young people
Information from the interviews carried out with African-Caribbean young people and with professionals suggests that the family contexts

which contribute to running away are broadly similar for these young people as for white young people.

To a certain extent, this is also true with respect to the information we have gathered on young people of Indian/Pakistani/Bangladeshi origin. The stereotype of young people fleeing arranged marriages is not a prominent issue. One professional commented:

> *I get a lot of that when I go out and talk about my project. People say, 'What's the main reason, is it arranged marriage?', and I say, 'There is a difference between arranged marriage and forced'. At the end of the day, that reason for leaving is right at the bottom.*

Some specific contextual factors relating to Asian young people which were more commonly mentioned for the 16- to 17-year-old age group are discussed in Chapter 10.

THE SUBSTITUTE CARE CONTEXT

All of the previous UK research on running away has highlighted young people running away from substitute care as an important issue. A number of studies (see Chapter 1) have found that young people who live in substitute care are more likely to run away than young people living with their family and our survey confirmed this. Young people currently living in foster or residential care were much more likely than average to have run away, with around 45% of both groups having run away overnight, compared to the rate for young people living with families of around 9.5%. Similarly, of the larger group (including the above) who had ever been in care, 30% had run away overnight. Young people who had spent time in substitute care were more likely to have run away more times (not necessarily from care). Almost a third (32%) of this small group had run away more than three times, compared to 13% of the remainder of the sample.

At the same time, running away from care probably accounts for a relatively small proportion of all running away. The vast majority (96%) of young people in the survey had run away from the family on the most recent occasion, and only 3.4% had run away from substitute care – foster care (2.1%) and children's homes (1.3%).

This issue is clearly rather a complex one, and it is easy to draw inappropriate conclusions from the data. For example, it is incorrect to equate the proportion who have been in care with the proportion who have run away from care. In the running-away sample from the survey, over half of those young people who had been in care at some point nevertheless ran away from their family on the most recent occasion, and over a third of these had only run away once. Similarly, only around half of those young people currently living in care who had experience of running away had run away from substitute care on the most recent occasion.

It is also important to recognise that young people living in care are not a randomly selected group. The majority will already have experienced the kind of family contexts described earlier in this chapter which make running away more likely. Therefore, it is inappropriate to see the high rate of running away from substitute care as necessarily being a negative reflection on the care system. Previous research has suggested that a substantial proportion of those young people who do run away from substitute care have started running away from their family before ever being looked after by the local authority.

Running away from substitute care was the subject of a large Department of Health funded research project (Wade *et al.*, 1998), the findings of which we have already outlined in Chapter 1. Prior to the current research project, it was probably the most extensively researched aspect of running away. It seemed therefore that we would be able to add relatively little to the knowledge on this particular area. However, one limitation of the above study was that it focused on young people who are currently living in substitute care. Since many young people move in and out of care, often spending only relatively short periods there, we are able to offer a fresh perspective on how the experience of being in care interacts with other aspects of these young people's lives in terms of running away.

In our purposive interview sample. the majority of young people (31 out of 52) who had first run away before the age of 16 had some experience of living in care. However, in over half of these cases the young person had run away before ever being placed in care.

BEING IN CARE BEFORE RUNNING AWAY BEGAN

For those young people who had been in care before starting to run away there were two groups:

• young people who had first run away whilst in care;

• young people who had first run away after returning home from care.

Most of the young people in the first group were in foster care at the time they first ran away and had been in care from a young age. Although there is a general tendency to view running away from care as to do with peers (this was the most common issue mentioned in interviews with professionals), for these particular young people there were often more fundamental issues. Some wanted to return home to live with their family and ran away in order to do this; others were unhappy about the decisions that were being made about them in care (including decisions about adoption or changes of placement). As we have already suggested, these were also usually young people with very troubled family backgrounds. All of these young people had experience of one or more of the following before being 'looked after': sexual abuse, bereavement of a parent, parents with serious alcohol or drug problems, and abandonment by a parent. Their running away needs to be viewed in this context rather than simply as a product of being in care. Young people in this group tended not to have positive feelings about either the process of being taken into care or their experiences of living there:

> I didn't understand. Ran up to attic and locked myself in. I was thinking, 'Where am I? Where's my mum?' At that age, I was too young to understand anything. All I wanted to do was to get away.

> Horrible, very violent. I witnessed a lot of adults being put in hospital, one even losing her eye. At the age of four, I didn't really understand it. I do now have a very violent temper. Being a kid, you do mimic what other people do.

Amongst the second group of young people who had been in care but first ran away after returning home, some had only been in care for a short while at a very young age or for a respite stay:

> It was only really just to give my mum a rest and stuff.

Others ran away at the point when they returned home from care, and subsequently went back into care. For these young people also, the family context was highly problematic and was the main contributory factor to running away.

BEING IN CARE AFTER RUNNING AWAY BEGAN

Most of the young people who lived in substitute care after running away began only did so for a year or two, either because they were approaching 16 when they started living in care or because they returned home to their family at some point. Again, some young people only lived in care for brief respites:

> *Because my mam and dad couldn't cope with me and needed a break.*

For these young people who moved into care after their first experience of running away, there were generally more positive experiences than for the group who had been looked after from a young age:

> *They* [foster carers] *were the best thing that ever happened to me.*

> *I got used to being there. I was a right bitch for the first four months and then they said I could go home if I was good for the next five months, so I was good for the next five months and I felt great when I got to go home. But I did miss my friends and some of the staff I liked because they were really supportive. I missed my mum, but I liked it in there in a way because I was safe. I wasn't getting lashed out at all the time.*

The comparison between family and care, and the respite from abuse mentioned in the last quote, was a theme for a number of the young people:

> *Well my dad is a divvy. He's always been in prison, so it might have been worse if I hadn't been in care. And he would probably still have been hitting me and that ... I never used to get hit and that whilst I was in care. I think there should be more foster parents so they don't get put into children's homes until they are 12 or 13.*

SUMMARY

A key finding in this chapter is that young people who live in step-families or with a lone parent are significantly more likely to run away than those living with both birth parents. This remains true even when economic factors are taken into account.

Additionally, and independently of the above, young people who ran away had significantly more negative views of the quality of their relationship with their parents.

Thus, the research suggests that poor family relationships make running away more likely irrespective of family form, but that there are additional stresses of living in families where changes in form have taken place which also make running away more likely. This conclusion was supported by the views of professionals interviewed for the research.

For young people who run away repeatedly, there is evidence of particularly high levels of family disruption and problems.

We have also looked at young people's experience of substitute care in this chapter. Young people who are currently living in substitute care are much more likely to have run away than young people living with family. Young people's reasons for running away from care included wanting to return home and unhappiness about the decisions being made about them. However, this is a complex area and, for most young people who run away and spend time in substitute care, their experience of substitute care is only one aspect of the context which contributes to their running away. It is inappropriate simply to view these young people as running away from care.

CHAPTER 6

The wider context

In this chapter, we consider the way in which issues such as offending, problems with drugs and alcohol, unhappiness and depression, and relationships with peers contribute to the overall context of running away.

We also consider some of the wider issues which may be relevant to or related to running away under the age of 16. These include the school context, the community or cultural context within which young people live, and structural factors which may have an influence on the likelihood of young people running away.

Finally, we consider the evidence on interventions by agencies in young people's lives before running away began.

THE PERSONAL CONTEXT

The survey contained a checklist of ten questions about young people's lives which give some insights into personal contextual factors. Young people were asked to tick any items which they felt were problems for them at the moment.

All ten items proved to be significant discriminators between those who had run away overnight and those who had not (i.e. had either never run away or had only run away during the day). Table 6.1 compares the proportion of each group who ticked each item.

As can be seen from Table 6.1, problems with drugs, problems with alcohol, and getting in trouble with the police were particularly strong discriminators. Around a third of the young people with each of these issues had run away overnight.

There were significant gender differences in the survey sample as a whole in the answers to all of the questions (except for 'other problems'). Females were much more likely than males to tick the first six categories and males were much more likely than females to tick categories seven to nine. This could be due to gender differences in willingness to admit to vulnerable feelings such as feeling lonely or feeling bad about oneself. Despite these gender differences, each of the items was significantly associated with running away for both genders with the exception of 'feeling under pressure' for females. Females who identified themselves as having problems with alcohol, drugs or offending were the group most highly likely to run away (with running away rates of 43%, 36% and 37% for the three issues respectively).

Table 6.1 *Relation between young people's problems and whether or not they had run away overnight*

Survey question	Had not run away overnight	Had run away overnight
Feeling fed up/depressed	32%	55%
Feeling under pressure	33%	40%
Feeling lonely	11%	25%
Not feeling good about yourself	24%	39%
Worried about the future	38%	46%
Problems with boy/girlfriends	17%	35%
Problems with drugs	4%	19%
Problems with alcohol	6%	25%
Getting in trouble with the police	6%	21%
Other problems	8%	19%

In general, the above findings suggest that young people with troubled lives are more likely to run away overnight. However, these findings must be viewed as indicative rather than conclusive because it was not possible in the survey to establish the chronology of different events. We do not know whether the above were issues before the young people started running away. It is equally possible that the problems started after running away began, and even that they could be a result of running away.

The detailed analysis of the purposive sample of interviews with young people enabled us to explore the chronology of different issues with a reasonable amount of accuracy (although there are inevitably doubts here about the extent to which the research participants were able to remember the timing of specific events).

In the remainder of this section, we explore the evidence from this analysis and also summarise relevant comments from the interviews with professionals.

ALCOHOL ISSUES

The evidence we have been able to gather suggests that alcohol use by young people under 16 is a small but noteworthy contextual factor linked to running away. Some professionals cited problems with alcohol as contextual factors linked to young people under 16 running away.

In the purposive interview sample, around a sixth of the young people talked about alcohol use as a serious problem for them. Usually, this had begun before they started running away and therefore can be regarded as contextual. It also led to other issues, including stealing in order to obtain the money to buy alcohol, being thrown out of home due to the alcohol use, and having a disrupted education. One interviewee explained how serious involvement with alcohol from the age of 12 had led him into violent behaviour and theft to support his drinking and described how:

When I drink, I think I'm Tarzan only a little bit harder!

DRUGS ISSUES

The issue of drugs use came over as an important contextual factor related to running away in the interviews with professionals and young people. As we have seen, a high proportion of young people in the survey who said they had drugs problems also had experience of running away. However, it is less clear to what extent the drugs use preceded the onset of running away.

A small number of professionals were aware of drugs use as an issue which led to young people running away, either due to the resulting problems at home or due to drug-related debts. One professional gave the example of how parents, confronted with the drug use of their child, feel:

> *They can't cope with what their children are getting involved with and that basically they have no control.*

In the purposive interview, a large minority of young people had experienced drug-related problems. The most common drugs used were cannabis and amphetamines, but a small number had taken heroin. A few of the young people interviewed mentioned issues around drugs as a reason for them being forced to leave home.

One interviewee who was using crack cocaine at the age of 12 described how she would run away to engage in housebreaking to pay for drugs. The drugs made her feel indestructible:

> *I always felt safe and, I mean, most of the time I was off my face I couldn't have been harmed by anyone. It's like a power trip when you're on drugs.*

However, in general, it was very difficult to establish the timing of events with respect to this issue and so it is not possible to identify the extent to which drugs usage preceded running away. There was substantial evidence of young people stealing in order to obtain the money to buy drugs and some evidence of drug-related issues contributing to detachment from the education system through truanting, suspension or exclusion.

OFFENDING

Offending is another factor mentioned by some professionals as a potential reason for young people running away under the age of 16, either due to the reaction of parents or in order to avoid the consequences:

> *When it comes to court to be remanded or bailed, parents refuse to have them home.*

Amongst the purposive interview sample of young people, offending arose as an issue in about a third of cases. One instance where the consequences of offending led to an interviewee running away was related as follows:

When I was 14/15, I used to get into trouble a lot, I got in with the wrong crowd and me and me dad had a big argument and started fist fighting. I were really badly beaten up and I left that night and I didn't come back for two week.

However, not all of this incidence preceded running away, and more regularly it was linked either to drug or alcohol use or as a means of survival once the young person had run away.

MENTAL HEALTH ISSUES

Young people's mental health is a difficult area to explore in research terms, not least due to difficulties of definition.

Only a small number of professionals mentioned young people's mental health issues as a contextual factor for running away under the age of 16. Most comments were focused on the over-16 age group. Nevertheless, one residential child care officer suggested the importance of recognising that some children under 16 suffer from depression and that this may contribute to their running away:

There should be more recognition that children suffer from depression. ...These young people who are depressed tend to run but they don't tend to go for as long an amount of time, more wandering around more than with any purpose.

For the purposive sample of young people, around one in six young people who had first run away under 16 mentioned mental-health related issues. Young people spoke of mental health issues in two main ways. First, a number of young people interviewed, predominantly female, spoke of depression or said that they had had a 'nervous breakdown'. Other young people, predominantly male, spoke of difficulties in managing their anger, some of which spilled over into violence. Both of these issues were often contextual factors which seemed to have contributed to young people running away. An interviewee who described himself as having a problem of 'anger management' recalled his feelings at the age of nine:

They're [the family are] all arguing and I don't want to get involved. So I would sit in my room and cry. There would be rows.

I would go to school the next day and someone would say something I didn't like and I would run round and hit 'em and then run off.

SEXUALITY

In the interviews with professionals, four workers mentioned sexuality as an issue for young people under 16 running away.

Amongst the interview sample, one young person who had run away under the age of 16 discussed his homosexuality as an issue and this was one of a complex set of factors, including violent behaviour and mental health issues, which led to the young person being forced to leave home at the age of 15.

This data is not particularly conclusive but does not suggest that issues around gay, lesbian or bisexuality are a major contextual factor for large numbers of young people under 16 running away. However, more specific research with gay, lesbian and bisexual young people may be a more productive way of exploring the links between their sexuality and any experience of running away.

SPECIAL NEEDS

In the survey sample, we explored special needs in two ways. First, young people in the mainstream school sample were asked if they felt they had any difficulties in learning. Around 10% of the total sample said they did have difficulties in learning, and the rate of running away was significantly higher for this group of young people than for the remainder of the sample. Almost one in six (16%) of these young people had run away overnight.

In view of the fact that many young people with special needs are not in mainstream schooling, the second way in which we explored running away for this group was to undertake a survey of special needs schools for young people with mild to moderate disabilities. Ultimately, we only achieved a sample size of 67 young people in six schools. This is too small a sample to enable us to draw definitive conclusions. However, the rate of running away was around 33% amongst this group of young people, which again suggests that young people with special needs are more likely than average to run away.

The small number of professionals who mentioned special needs as a contextual factor in terms of running away tended to focus on behavioural difficulties as the main issue. For instance, a social services after-care worker suggested that, in the case of behavioural difficulties:

Maybe parents become less tolerant or maybe the difficulties become increased... of course, young people are getting bigger at 15/16 as well. So their physical size – the behaviours that were exhibited at 7,8 and 9 become a little less acceptable in the house at 14, 15, 16.

A few of the interview sample mentioned that they had been diagnosed as having special needs. In most cases, this was related to dyslexia, although it does not appear that this was diagnosed until the young people had left school. An interviewee related how they regretted that this was the case:

It's only about two months ago I found out that I'm dyslexic. In school, I just couldn't get my head into the books, that's why it didn't get any further. At school they didn't know anything about it.

Although we have been unable to explore the relationship between special needs and running away in great detail, our findings suggest a probable link between the two issues which would warrant further more specific investigation.

RELATIONSHIPS WITH PEERS

Young people's relationships with peers become an increasingly important sphere of their life as young people mature. It is natural, then, to examine the influence that peer relationships have on the incidence of running away. In the USA, research has suggested that the nature and quality of peer relationships can be an important contextual factor in terms of running away (Brennan *et al.*, 1978).

There are a number of possible ways in which peer relationships might influence the likelihood of running away. First, there may be peer pressure to run away; it may be an accepted or valued behaviour amongst certain peer groups. Second, young people may run away to accompany friends who do so. Third, strong positive relationships with peers may lead to problems between the young person and parents which may in turn lead to the young person choosing to leave or being forced to leave. Fourth, negative relationships with peers may contribute to young people wanting to escape their current context. We found some evidence of all four of these links within the data gathered.

Only a small number of the professionals focused on peer relationships as a context for running away. There were suggestions here that peer pressure and finding a space to share with peers may both sometimes contribute to young people running away.

Despite the low profile of this issue amongst professionals, the data gathered from young people suggests that the peer context may be quite significant.

The survey included a question about whether the young person's friends had ever run away. The answers to this question confirm the widespread nature of running away, and the fact that it is not an invisible issue amongst young people. Overall, over two-fifths (42%) of the young people surveyed said that they had a friend who had run away. Young people who had themselves run away were much more likely to have a friend who had run away (80%) than those who had not run away (38%).

We have also already seen (in Chapter 4) that around one in 12 young people in the survey mentioned peer factors amongst their reasons for running away.

The interviews with young people enabled us to explore relationships with peers in more detail. It seems from these interviews that peer relationships are not an important contextual factor for those young people who start running away before secondary school age. However, for those who started running away between the ages of 11 and 15, they are more significant. Around one in five of our purposive interview sample mentioned peer factors as contextual to their running away. Commonly, these young people became involved in drugs or alcohol use around the ages of 11 to 12. In some cases, this had led to the young person becoming involved in offending. These issues had then led to the young person running away or to a deterioration of relationships with parents which led to their being forced to leave. For instance, one interviewee related:

I was 14 at the time. I was going in drunk and arguing with everybody all the time. I was kicked out of the house. My pals were older than me and I wanted to be with them. I wouldn't go to school 'cause my friends had all left.

THE SCHOOL CONTEXT

Previous research has suggested that there is a link between detachment from school and running away. In the UK, Rees (1993) found that young people who said that they regularly truanted from school were significantly more likely than other young people to run away. Stein *et al.* (1994) found that young people who were 'on the streets' had often become detached from school at a relatively young age. In the USA, Brennan *et al.* (1978) found that loose attachment to school and negative experiences of school were both linked to increased likelihood of running away.

The professionals interviewed as part of the current research project suggested that, for the under-16 age group, school factors may relate to running away in a number of ways. The link between non-attendance or exclusion and running away was mentioned; bullying at school and parental pressure in relation to school achievement were both cited as factors which could lead to young people running away; and, for young people approaching 16 years of age, the possibility of decisions about leaving school contributing to arguments at home was raised.

The survey showed a strong link between problems at school and running away. Young people who said they truanted from school were much more likely than other young people to have run away. Nearly a third (31%) of those who often truanted and more than two-fifths (22%) of those who sometimes truanted had run away overnight, compared to 6% of those who had never truanted. Similarly, young people who had been excluded from school were significantly more likely to have run away than other young people. A quarter of this group had run away overnight on at least one occasion.

In general, young people who had run away overnight expressed more negative views of school than other young people. Thirty-six per cent of these young people said that they did not like school, compared to 17% of young people who had not run away overnight.

There was also a significant link between persistent bullying at school and running away. Twenty-three per cent of those who said they had often been bullied at school had run away.

Finally, in our small sub-sample of 60 young people attending pupil referral units around two-fifths of these young people had run away from home.

The interviews with young people confirm the above findings for those who have run away regularly. Around half of the purposive sample had spent time away from school through truancy, suspension, or exclusion or had left school early. As one interviewee succinctly put it:

I never really got into trouble at school because I was never there.

As with other contextual factors, it is difficult to establish the exact chronology of events and it is likely that running away and problems at school are intertwined rather than one factor causing the other. However, in a number of cases, it seems that running away and being away from school (through truancy or exclusion) went hand-in-hand. In two cases, young people who had run away before the age of 11 had also been permanently excluded from primary school.

Surprisingly, given this overall context, some young people expressed strong positive feelings about their school experience, including one young person who saw it as a refuge from home. However, the majority expressed a strong antipathy to school, and there were also regular mentions of being bullied. One young person described how her difficulties were exacerbated by a sense of victimisation:

In school, all the teachers knew I had been abused. All the other kids knew also and boys shouted at me. I used to get tripped up at school. So I left in the third year.

Finally, the young people who took part in interviews were asked whether they had obtained any qualifications at school. The information here is incomplete, but at least two-fifths had left school without any GCSEs.

THE COMMUNITY/CULTURAL CONTEXT

In most of the areas where we contacted agencies, the professionals we spoke to touched on specific community or cultural issues which they felt had a bearing on running away in their areas. Most often these linked relationships within families to the wider social systems of which they were a part.

In relation to African-Caribbean and Asian young people, a

number of viewpoints were expressed. Most professionals who had involvement with young people from minority ethnic communities felt that running away was not uncommon, although it might be more hidden, and that the reasons for running away were broadly similar to those for white young people. Amongst the under-16s, physical and emotional abuse and conflict with parents or step-parents figured prominently. For older Asian teenagers, an additional ingredient centred on perceived over-restrictive parenting, parental rejection of boyfriends or girlfriends and, in a minority of cases, the threat of forced marriage.

A common professional view was that, while the reasons for running were broadly similar across all ethnic groups, their experiences once missing could be divergent. As one professional put it:

> The situation is very similar and the reasons for leaving home are very similar to their white counterparts. But then it's the difficulties they face afterwards, because of the colour of their skin, because of their culture, because of how they dress or whatever. That's where the main problems arise.

It was generally felt that African-Caribbean and Asian young people tended to avoid city centres and the streets in general (and the mainstream agencies that are based there) because they are too hostile. It was suggested that African-Caribbean young people tend to rely more heavily on extended family members and friends for help at these times. Asian young people, in contrast, fearful of the loss of community respect (*'izzat'*) that may accrue to themselves and their families as a consequence of running away, may be less likely to turn to wider kin, and either continue coping with a difficult home situation in private or make a more premeditated escape, often further away from home. One professional said:

> From my experience of working with [Asian] young people who have been involved in homelessness, they have had to move...to the other end of the city or to a different city altogether. That's what I mean by it being planned in terms of it being quite a clear decision.

Evidence from both Asian young people and professionals also suggested that running away, especially for females seeking relationships of their choosing, risked a more final separation from family and community. The loss of face experienced by their family within the community could inhibit the possibilities of a negotiated return.

African-Caribbean and Asian young people were also considered less likely to access those mainstream services that exist. Factors inhibiting them from approaching such services included concerns about the predominantly 'white' nature of these services and the racism that might result, a perceived lack of cultural awareness and sensitivity amongst agency workers, and perhaps also a failure of agencies to provide the right kinds of services or to publicise them amongst minority ethnic communities in an appropriate way. As one professional suggested:

> *I believe that a lot of people might not fit in with the existing services. For example, they might go to a rehab centre or a refuge, they may go to any of these existing services and they will not fit in because their identity is different. So the existing services might not be able to cater for them completely and, if we have nothing else as back-up, what else is there for these young people?*

Some of these issues were also mentioned in relation to other cultural groups – the Welsh-speaking community in Gwynedd, the Chinese community in Plymouth, the Orthodox Jewish and Yemeni communities in Salford, the Somalian community in Cardiff, and the divided communities in Strabane. For all of these groups, there was a view that young people were more likely to attempt to resolve problems within their community and less likely to access generic services.

Linked to the above point, there was a view that young people in some or all of these communities were less likely to sleep rough when they ran away. We did not find any evidence to support such an argument in the survey data. There was no significant difference between the rates of sleeping rough for young people of different ethnic origins.

In the interviews with young people, there were some mentions of a feeling of safety or of extensive support networks in rural and suburban areas, although there were also comments about the restrictions and lack of anonymity in these areas. For instance, an interviewee who at 15 went to live with an older man now no longer feels able to return to her small village:

My friends disowned me because I was living with an older man. And like now I won't go back to [my village] *because of what all the people I knew said about me with that man so... They all know everything.*

There appears to be both a negative and a positive side to close-knit communities as far as young people are concerned.

THE STRUCTURAL CONTEXT

The link between structural issues, such as economic disadvantage and poor housing conditions, is worthy of exploration because these factors may form part of the backdrop to the issues which lead to young people running away. Earlier research (Rees, 1993) found a link between economic disadvantage and running away in a sample of young people in Leeds.

The sampling strategy for our survey ensured that we achieved a good mix of areas on the basis of economic indicators. The task of obtaining information about family economic status from young people through a self-completed questionnaire is a difficult one. It is not possible, for example, to gather information about parents' occupation or income with any degree of accuracy. We utilised two measures in the survey designed to identify young people living in low income families – the number of adults in the household in paid employment, and whether the young person received free school meals. These two measures have been used previously and have proved reliable indicators as far as they go, although clearly they do not provide any element of gradation amongst families above a certain economic level.

Both of the above measures were related to the incidence of young people running away. Amongst the relatively small proportion (one in 14) of young people who lived in a household where no-one had a paid job, the rate of running away overnight was 17%. Rather more young people (one in eight) received free school meals and around 15% of this group had run away. There is evidence here, then, of a significant link between economic disadvantage and running away, at least in families at the lower end of the income distribution.

We went on to analyse the links between economic disadvantage, family form and running away. This seemed pertinent because Rees

(1993) found that, in Leeds, when economic factors were taken into account, the rate of running away in lone-parent families was no higher than in families with two birth parents, although the higher rate in step-families was statistically significant.

However, our analysis with this much larger and more wide-reaching sample gives different conclusions. We found that, when economic status was taken into account, the differences in rates of running away for different family forms changed little and remained significant. However, when family form was taken into account, the link between economic disadvantage and running away was weakened and was no longer at a level which could be regarded as statistically significant. Whilst this finding may seem rather obscure, it carries important messages. What it suggests is that, whilst lone-parent families and step-families are likely to be poorer than families with both birth parents, and are likely to evidence higher rates of running away, there is no direct link between economic disadvantage and running away.

This suggests that running away may be more closely linked to the emotional and relationship issues experienced by young people in families than by the level of prosperity or poverty within the family. It also suggests that running away cannot be seen as an issue which is predominantly about low-income households. There is clearly a considerable incidence of running away in wealthier families and, where there are difficulties in relation to family form or family relationships, these are equally likely to lead to young people running away. Another way of looking at the findings is that the link between economic disadvantage and disrupted family forms means that poverty indirectly contributes towards the incidence of running away by contributing to family forms where running away is more likely. This is a plausible explanation, but it implies a causal link which it is beyond this research project to establish. Does poverty cause changes in family form, do changes in family form lead to poverty, or do the two go hand in hand in certain contexts?

Interestingly, the professionals interviewed for the research did not focus greatly on economic factors when explaining the contexts which they felt influence young people running away under the age of 16 (although the picture for 16- to 17-year-olds is very different as we shall see in Chapter 10).

However, there were two other structural issues which were mentioned by a small number of professionals. First, some workers were aware of households where overcrowding had created tensions which ultimately led to young people running away either by choice or out of necessity. Second, a few workers highlighted the fact that the laws relating to young people under the age of 16 who are away from home (as outlined in Chapter 1) could be a barrier to agencies providing services for this group, thus exacerbating any problems which the young people were facing.

AGENCY INTERVENTIONS

Finally, in terms of context, we examine young people's involvement with helping agencies before and after they first ran away.

Due to space considerations and difficulties in formulating and piloting appropriate questions, we did not gather information on this topic through the survey questionnaire. So we are reliant here on the information from interviews with young people.

INTERVENTIONS BEFORE RUNNING AWAY STARTED

Nine of the purposive sample of 52 young people who had run away before the age of 16 had started running away from substitute care and a further five ran away after returning home from care. Clearly, these 14 young people had all had social work intervention prior to running away.

Of the remaining 38 young people, there is evidence of at least 11 who had involvement with a social worker before running away, and a further five who may have had some involvement. Thus, less than half of the young people who had not been in care had had involvement with social services.

There is very little evidence of any involvement with other services before running away, although two young people had had involvement with the police – one due to being sexually abused and the case going to court, and one due to offending which went to court (presumably, the probation service was also involved here, although this was not mentioned by the young person). Finally, two young people had involvement with mental health services.

In terms of young people's views of these interventions, there were mixed feelings about social workers, with some young people expressing strong dislike and others being very positive. The two young people who had had mental health service involvement were negative about it, although this is hardly conclusive evidence.

Whilst we need to bear in mind that this was not a representative sample in any way, the above clearly illustrates the possibility that young people who run away have had no agency interventions before being away. It seems that this was the case for slightly more than half of the young people interviewed who had not lived in substitute care prior to running away.

INTERVENTIONS AFTER RUNNING AWAY STARTED

There was much more evidence of agencies becoming involved in young people's lives after running away had started. Forty-six out of the 52 young people in the purposive sample had had involvement with at least one agency in relation to problems they were facing, and some had been in touch with as many as five or six different agencies.

Social workers

Social workers were by far the most common professionals for young people to mention. Most (36) of the young people in the purposive sample had some contact with social services under the age of 16.

Not surprisingly, given the role and responsibilities of social workers, young people had mixed feelings about their involvement with them:

> *Some were real canny but some were real divvies.*

Young people particularly valued social workers who were accessible to them:

> *Since I was three, I've had loads of social workers – too many to remember. I can normally pick up when I first meet them whether I'm gonna like them or not – the one I have now, I like her – she's brilliant. Whenever I have the need, I can contact her any time during office hours and my foster mum has a number that I can use any time if needed.*

Two problems commented upon by several young people were the often temporary nature of social workers' involvement and a feeling of not being able to relate to them:

I've had loads of social workers and key workers and leaving care scheme workers and what have you, but they eventually leave you alone as well... you know what I mean. They're all enthusiastic in the beginning: 'Oh, I'll help you out with this and that', and then they slowly fade away, lose contact with you.

No offence, but she's English and well, well posh... And everything's always got to go the way she wants it.

Despite some of these difficulties, there were a number of examples of social workers' interventions being valued by young people and effective in helping them with the problems they were facing:

They've helped me find somewhere to stay and given me money when I've needed it. In fact, I'd recommend Social Services to anyone.

The police
The police were the next most commonly mentioned professionals. Nine young people had had contact with them in connection with having run away. Again, there were both positive and negative views, at least partly stemming from the role and responsibility of the police in terms of young people who run away:

The police were really nice to me at first and then they got annoyed. They had so many forms to fill in. I know every policeman where I was, that's how bad it got. I'm not proud of that.

An important issue in connection with the police was young people's desire to be listened to and believed:

I never wanted to live with my mum because my step-dad used to beat me up. I told my auntie who's a police officer but nothing happened about it. She believed me. I was interviewed by the police but I guess they believed my mum and step-dad over me.

Other interventions
Interventions by other professionals appear to have been relatively rare for this sample of young people.

One young person mentioned a youth worker:

I like my key worker, he listens to me.

Five young people mentioned seeing a counsellor, psychiatrist or psychologist in connection with their problems. In some cases, the young person valued this involvement. One young person, who had seen a counsellor from the age of 13, commented as follows:

I was with her for at least three years and she was brilliant, and you know she helped me through my boyfriend situation where at 16 I got in with him and he was a bit... I was looking for the love that I never had at home basically, the love that I wanted I didn't have, so I looked for it somewhere else, which was with him... I wanted the comfort love, you know the cwches [hugs] and the kisses and stuff like that ...and it's still not right now between my mother and myself.

The work of a psychologist was also found helpful by one young person:

I went from being really fat and not looking after myself to something looking more human and looking after myself.

However, not all young people found these kinds of 'talking' interventions useful. One young person who had been referred to a psychiatrist described her experience as follows:

All I did was sit there and look at the clock, because basically the way he was trying to get things out of me wasn't the right way of doing it, because I was very young and I think you've got to understand what they are feeling really, whereas I think he got it out of a book.

Finally, the potential value of educational initiatives was illustrated by one young person's recollection of an NSPCC education worker visiting her school. This young person had been regularly physically abused by her mother, who had a serious drink problem, from the age of five:

I remember seeing all this stuff about a little girl. I didn't know where to put myself. Everybody had tears in their eyes because the stories we[re] so horrible, like the ones the NSPCC have got now; that triggers me off a lot... I walked up to this woman, she had this picture, 'I want to talk to you a minute', then I said, 'It doesn't matter' and walked off. I walked away with tears in my eyes, all these pictures everywhere, and we had to collect money for them, so it was like 'Oh well'.

Whilst this young person was unable immediately to talk about her feelings, it is easy to see how these kinds of initiatives can raise young people's awareness and give them encouragement to seek help with problems they are facing.

SUMMARY

In this chapter, we have examined the links between running away and a number of issues in young people's lives: offending, alcohol and drug use, mental health issues, relationships with peers, and problems at school. In most cases, there are significant links between the issues, with young people who run away being more likely to experience problems in all of the above mentioned areas. What is less clear is the extent to which the occurrence of these issues either precedes or post-dates the first time when young people run away, and to what extent a problem or issue in one area causes a problem or issue in another. It seems unlikely that there is any clear progression of events, and it is more plausible that these issues represent a matrix where any one issue can spark off others. The research has provided illustrations of examples where offending or drugs use precedes running away and is to some extent a causal factor. On the other hand, there are examples of running away leading to drugs use or offending in order to survive. There are also more complex links. For example, peers may introduce a young person to drugs, using drugs may lead to offending in order to obtain money, and then parental reactions to the young person's offending may lead to them running away or being forced to leave. The links between these problematic issues that young people face suggest the need for links to be made at the policy and practice level. There may be a danger of young people becoming 'locked in' to one or more of the specific agency systems such as youth justice or mental health and becoming labelled as having a specific problem.

We have also looked at several other aspects of young people's lives. First, considering the cultural context within which young people grow up, it seems that for certain groups, notably including young people of African-Caribbean and Asian origin, there are specific cultural factors which may have an impact both on the likelihood of running away and its significance to the young person.

Second, we found that there appears not to be a direct link between economic factors and running away. Young people living in a particular family form are roughly equally likely to run away, irrespective of the economic status of that family.

Finally, we have looked at agency interventions in young people's lives both before and after they start to run away. It is probably true to say that a majority of young people who run away have no specific interventions relating to problems they are facing before they start running away. There is evidence of a more extensive level of intervention once running away has started, primarily involving social workers and police.

7

Experiences and patterns of being away

In this chapter, we will look at two aspects of young people being away from home under the age of 16. First, we will look overall at young people's experience of being away. Then, we will look at patterns of running away and whether the research provides evidence of a developing pattern as young people run away more often.

EXPERIENCES OF BEING AWAY

LENGTH OF TIME AWAY

Just under a third of the young people did not spend a night away from home on the most recent occasion when they ran away. A further third only spent one night away. Approximately one in seven spent a week or more away.

There was no difference by sex or type of area either in terms of the proportion of young people who were away overnight or the lengths of times that young people spent away.

There was no significant difference in the proportion of young people from different ethnic groups who ran away overnight. However, there were significant differences in terms of lengths of being away. Young people of African-Caribbean and Asian origins were more likely than young white people to run away for a longer period. Forty-one per cent of young people of African-Caribbean origin and 34% of young people of Indian/Pakistani/Bangladeshi origin had run away for a week or more on the most recent occasion, compared to 18% of white young people.

Finally, young people who had been forced to leave spent longer away than young people who had run away. Around two-fifths (41%) of young people who had been forced to leave spent a week or more away, compared to 8% of those who had run away.

WHERE THE YOUNG PEOPLE SLEPT

Two-fifths of the young people slept at a friend's on the most recent occasion that they ran away. A quarter slept with relatives, and a further quarter slept rough.

Males (33%) were more likely than females (20%) to sleep rough and somewhat less likely to stay with relatives.

There were no significant differences in where young people of different ethnic groups slept.

Neither were there any significant differences for types of area, although there was a marginal difference here, with young people in rural areas appearing to be the most likely to sleep rough and young people in London the least likely.

Perhaps surprisingly, those who had been forced to leave were significantly less likely to sleep rough and much more likely to go to relatives.

A multivariate analysis of gender, where slept and run away/being forced to leave suggests that both gender and whether forced to leave are significant influences on whether a young person sleeps rough. Thus, males who had run away were the most likely to sleep rough (36%), followed by females who had run away (22%), males who had been forced to leave (21%) and finally females who had been forced to leave (10%).

WHERE THE YOUNG PEOPLE WENT

Around a third of young people said they had gone out of their local area whilst they were away, with the proportion being higher for those who had been away overnight (40%). However, most of this travelling was quite local. Where the young person specified where they went, over three-fifths (62%) had remained within the same general area (e.g. county, city) and a further fifth (22%) outside cities had gone to a neighbouring city. This left only 16% — around 2.5% of the total runaway sample – who had gone further afield. Under half of these young people had gone to a large city (mainly London, Dublin, Glasgow and Birmingham). The majority had gone to coastal or smaller regional towns.

Males (45%) were significantly more likely to go outside the local area than females (35%).

There were no significant differences on the basis of ethnicity, running from family or care, whether run away or forced to leave, or type of area.

MEANS OF SURVIVAL

The questionnaire asked young people how they had survived whilst they were away on the most recent occasion that they ran away. For the majority of young people in the survey who ran away (those who returned the same day or stayed away for one night only), survival is not a big issue. The large majority of these young people either did not see the question as relevant or said that they managed fine with money or food they had taken with them or with the help of friends or relatives.

For the young people who stayed away two nights or more, the situation is more mixed. Over a third of the young people (35%) relied solely on relatives whilst away, a slightly lower proportion (28%) relied solely on friends, and 2% relied on both relatives and friends. A further 19% relied solely on food and money they had taken with them when they ran away or on money they received from part-time work.

Thus, the large majority of young people (84%) relied on informal support networks or their own means in order to survive whilst away. Of the remaining young people, the large majority (9% of those who had run away for two nights or more) survived by stealing. Less common strategies were begging (seven young people), rummaging in dustbins (five young people), using sex as a means of survival (five young people) and selling drugs (two young people).

In summary, then, over two-thirds of the young people who stayed away for two nights or more were supported by people, a sixth supported themselves in a relatively safe way, and around one in seven supported themselves in more unsafe ways.

Not surprisingly, the young people who were away longer were significantly more likely to resort to more risky means of survival, with a fifth of those who were away for a week or more having done so.

Additionally, those young people who slept rough were much more likely to resort to risky survival strategies. Over a third of these young people had used one of the strategies listed above, and the large majority of the remainder had survived solely on their own means (money they had taken with them). Only a fifth had support from relatives or friends whilst away.

Males (26%) were far more likely to use risky survival strategies than females (5%), although some of this difference is accounted for by males being more likely to sleep rough and stay away longer. Males were also more likely to rely on their own resources. Half of males (51%) got support from relatives or friends compared to 82% of the females.

GOOD AND BAD THINGS ABOUT BEING AWAY

Young people were asked a number of things about the most recent time when they were away. These questions were derived from earlier research (see Stein *et al.*, 1994). Table 7.1 shows the number of young people who ticked the 'Yes' box in response to each question.

Table 7.1 *Young people's views on being away*

Question about being away	% who said 'Yes'
1. Did being away give you time to think?	83%
2. Did it give you relief from pressure?	65%
3. Did you feel lonely?	39%
4. Were you hungry/thirsty?	23%
5. Were you frightened?	32%
6. Did you make friends?	36%
7. Were you happier than before?	40%
8. While you were away, were you physically hurt?	13%
9. While you were away, were you sexually assaulted?	8%
10. Did being away help you to sort out your problems?	54%

A minority of young people were physically hurt or sexually assaulted whilst they were away. The combined incidence for at least one of these two categories is 15% (around one in seven) of those who had run away overnight. For a larger proportion of young people, the experience was still a distressing one, with a quarter of the young people being hungry or thirsty and a third being frightened and feeling lonely.

On the other hand, there were clearly some positive aspects of running away for many of the young people. Five out of six young people felt that it had given them time to think, and over half had had relief from pressure and felt that it had helped them to sort out their problems.

Males were significantly more likely to have been hungry/thirsty, to have been physically hurt or to have been sexually assaulted. Females were significantly more likely to have felt frightened.

Young people who were away for longer were more likely to make friends, more likely to feel happier than before, and more likely to have been physically hurt or to have been sexually assaulted.

Young people who slept rough were more likely to have felt lonely, to have been hungry/thirsty, less likely to have made friends, more likely to have been physically hurt or sexually assaulted, and less likely to feel that running away had helped to sort out their problems.

Thus, there is a tendency for more negative experiences amongst males, those who were away longer and those who slept rough.

A multivariate analysis suggests that, although males were more likely to be hurt (physically or sexually) than females, gender is not directly related to whether a young person is physically hurt or sexually assaulted. Whether a young person sleeps rough and how long they are away are both linked to each other and to the likelihood of being hurt. It is the fact that males are more likely to sleep rough that makes them more vulnerable to being hurt, rather than their gender *per se*.

Young people who slept rough and spent a week or more away on the last occasion that they ran away had a 44% chance of being hurt. The next highest risk groups were those who slept rough and spent two to six nights away (29% were hurt) and those who did not sleep rough but spent a week or more away (16%).

Young people who did not sleep rough but slept with someone they had just met were also at a high risk of being hurt – 47% of this whole sub-group and 67% of those who spent more than a week away had been hurt.

Finally, in general, young people who stayed with relatives were the least likely to be hurt (8% overall) but those who only stayed one night were more likely to be hurt (12%) than those who stayed longer.

OUTCOMES OF RUNNING AWAY

The survey questionnaire included an open-ended question in relation to the most recent running away incident, 'What happened in the end?'. Two-thirds of the young people wrote responses to this question.

In terms of returning home or alternative resolutions of the incident, around two-thirds said that they had decided to go home. Quite often, young people gave reasons why they had chosen to go home and these broadly divided into two categories – the unpleasant nature of being away (cold, hungry, scared, and so on), and feelings about family (missing people, worrying about them, and so on).

> *I had a dream that my mother died of sadness and that made me realise how selfish I was being.*

From the data we have, it is not possible to estimate the prevalence of each of these categories, but they are both clearly common.

Amongst the young people who did not choose to return home voluntarily, most were found and returned home by family (16% of those who responded), police (9%), or unspecified (3%).

This leaves a small proportion who were either persuaded or forced to go home by other people who intervened (for example the parents of friends who a young person was staying with), found a place to live elsewhere (usually with a relative), or were still currently away from home.

Young people's responses also touch on two other issues. First, regarding the reactions of parents, there is insufficient data for a detailed analysis but positive (relief, apologies, etc.) and negative reactions (punishment, violence, shouting) were both common.

Second, a number of young people commented on what happened regarding the problems that had caused them to run away, after they returned. Some young people noted that the problems had subsequently been resolved and they now felt better about things.

> *My mum and I sat down and talked and sorted some of the problems out.*

> *In the end, my mum found me and made me feel a lot better. Four years later my mother left him* [step-father].

Others commented that nothing had changed in the situation or that it had deteriorated further:

> *Nothing changed, it just got worse. So I took an overdose, unfortunately it didn't work.*

> *I went home and I'm still struggling now.*

PATTERNS OF BEING AWAY

We now go on to examine the evidence regarding whether the above experiences change as young people are away more often. We begin by examining in some detail the first experience of being away, and then go on to compare these experiences with those of young people who run away on more than one occasion.

FIRST INCIDENTS

Evidence from the survey

In the survey questionnaire, the questions about running-away behaviour related to the most recent incident of running away. Thus, for young people who had run away a number of times, we do not have any information about the first time they ran away apart from their age at the time. The data on age at first incident has already been presented in Chapter 3 – around 25% of the running away sample first ran away before the age of 11.

However, the survey does enable us to compare running-away behaviour for those young people who only ran away once, by the age at which they ran away.

Surprisingly, this analysis yields very few significant differences. Young people who first ran away before the age of 11 were less likely to stay away overnight (62% returned within the day, compared to 37% of older young people). However, for those young people who did stay away overnight, we found no significant difference between those who had run away before the age of 11 and older young people in terms of the length of time they spent away, where they slept, whether they went alone or with someone, whether they ran away or were forced to leave, or whether they were physically hurt or sexually assaulted whilst away. Whilst these differences were not significant, it is notable, for instance, that a higher (rather than lower) proportion of the younger group said they were physically hurt and/or sexually assaulted, and there was a marginally significant difference with more of the younger group sleeping rough.

Evidence from the interviews

As with the survey, it seems that a higher proportion of the younger age group did not stay out overnight on the first occasion. However, for those young people who did spend at least one night away, there were no particularly noticeable patterns in terms of length of time away, with a fairly even distribution over a wide range from one night to a week or more.

Around half of the young people slept rough on this first occasion. This is considerably higher than for the survey sample. For most of the young people sleeping rough was a very unpleasant experience. One of the interviewees described his experience of sleeping rough as follows:

> *When it was raining and I was sleeping on the streets, I would get up and be really cold, shivering and I couldn't move sometimes, my feet would be stuck.*

Places where young people slept included derelict houses, bus and train stations, parks, back alleys and fields. This suggests that most of these young people would have been relatively invisible whilst away. The young people who did not sleep rough stayed mostly with friends, and in lesser numbers with relatives. Three young people slept in nightshelters or hostels (presumably lying about their age) but two of these felt so threatened in these places that they returned home. It is notable that, where a young person under the age of 11 spent at least one night away, they almost always slept rough. There are some tentative indications here of an age difference in terms of the likelihood of sleeping rough, which are consonant with the marginal differences in the survey findings presented above.

In order to survive, a number of young people resorted to stealing, begging or selling drugs to get the money and food to survive. For instance, one research participant who slept rough described how they would go 'shedding' (stealing from sheds) during the day and another admitted to:

> *Stealing cars, stealing anything to survive. I had nothing at all like.*

I stole anything to sell on to make money; anything and everything.

Only a few had taken any money with them when they had left home.

Around a third of the sample had received support from friends or family members and a slightly lower number received any professional support whilst away, although a few mentioned what they perceived as helpful interventions by social workers or police, including some who were placed in care as an alternative to returning home.

Most young people returned home of their own accord, whilst around one in five were found and returned by the police. From the young people's accounts, there were some concerning examples of young people being returned to physically abusive family environments without any substantial intervention.

Responses of parents varied considerably, but there were some indications that young people who had run away due to physical abuse were beaten again on returning home.

All in all, there were few age-related differences evident in the analysis of the interviews. Perhaps the only noticeable difference is some tentative support for the differences in triggers for running away highlighted in the survey sample.

Summary

In summary, the analysis presented above suggests that there is little or no difference in young people's first running away experience, according to the age when this occurs. However, for young people who subsequently run away on a number of occasions, there may well be some differences in both the triggers for running away (with higher rates of family conflict and physical abuse) and the risk levels whilst away (as evidenced by the proportion who slept rough). We will now build on these conclusions in going on to analyse the patterns of running away for those young people who run away on more than one occasion.

SUBSEQUENT INCIDENTS

We now address a key issue in understanding the phenomenon of young people running away or being forced to leave home under the age of 16 – whether there is evidence of a developing pattern of being away.

Evidence from the survey

In the survey, we gathered information only about the most recent occasion that each young person had run away. Thus, it is not possible to compare different running-away incidents for the same young person as it is for the interviews. However, we can examine some evidence of patterns of running away.

First, we compared the information about the most recent running-away incident according to the number of times young people had run away. This enables us to go some way towards examining the proposition that running-away patterns develop and change. If we found no difference between the behaviour of young people who had run away once or twice and those who had run away more often, it would undermine the idea of a developing running-away pattern.

However, a simple statistical analysis of running-away behaviour showed that there are many significant differences between young people's experiences of being away.

Young people who had run away more often were, on the most recent occasion:

- more likely to be forced to leave (29% of those who had run away more than three times);

- more likely to cite school, personal and other problems as reasons for running away;

- likely to spend more time away (34% of those who had run away more than three times had spent a week or more away on the most recent occasion);

- more likely to sleep rough (38%) or with a stranger (8%);

- more likely to use risky survival strategies such as stealing, begging or survival sex (29% of those who had run away more than three times adopted at least one of the risky strategies identified in Chapter 6);

- more likely to go out of the area (55%);

- more likely to be hungry/thirsty, physically hurt, and/or sexually assaulted whilst they were away;

- less likely to feel that being away had given them time to think.

There were other ways in which young people's behaviour or experience did not differ. In particular, there was no difference in terms of whether they ran away alone or with someone and no difference in terms of the proportion who cited problems at home as a reason for running away.

Of course, as we already indicated in the overview, some of the above tendencies will be related. The fact that young people who have run away more often tend to be away for longer and are more likely to sleep rough means that they are more at risk of being hurt whilst away.

IS THERE A DEVELOPING PATTERN OF RUNNING AWAY?

Whilst the above findings do not undermine the notion of a developing pattern of running away, they do not prove it either. There are at least two other plausible explanations for the findings.

First, it is possible that there is an age-related effect in that patterns change as young people get older. If this was the case, since young people who have run away more times may be more likely to have run away recently, whereas the young people who have run away only once will have been a range of ages when they ran away, the above link could be spurious. This possibility was examined by comparing those young people who had run away a number of times with those young people who had run away once after the age of 12. This served to exclude those young people who only ran away once at a fairly young age. However, this comparison failed to find significant differences. Earlier in this chapter we referred to analysis of experiences of running away for those young people who had only run away once according to the age when they had run away, and also found little evidence of an age-related effect. We can therefore be reasonably confident in discounting the possibility of an age-related effect. This in itself is a very interesting and somewhat surprising finding, as it would seem natural to assume that there would be considerable evidence of differences in running-away experiences and behaviour according to the age at which young people ran away. Our survey suggests that, by and large, this is not the case.

The second possible alternative explanation is that, rather than there being a developing pattern of running away whereby, for example, the more often the young person has run away the longer they stay away, in fact young people who run away often have always had the same behaviour, although this behaviour differs from those who do not run away often. Whilst this explanation may seem a little odd, it cannot be discounted entirely because it may be the severity of young people's problems at home which leads them to run away often, and this same severity may also lead to a consistently risky pattern of running away from the outset.

The survey data cannot assist in examining this alternative hypothesis as we only have details about one running-away incident for each young person. However, we have gone some way towards examining it through a careful analysis of the interviews with young people, as with this data it was possible often to identify details of a number of running-away incidents in chronological order.

ANALYSIS OF INTERVIEWS WITH YOUNG PEOPLE
Number of times young people had run away
Around half of the purposive sample had run away on ten or more occasions. Of the remainder, a third had run away on at least five occasions and a third had run away only once or twice. The sample, therefore, is fairly heavily concentrated at the more serious end of the running away continuum, although this is helpful rather than a problem, given the broad overview provided by the survey data, which focuses more on young people who have run away once or twice. The majority (around two-thirds) of those young people who started running away under the age of 11 ran away on ten or more occasions and most of the remainder ran away on at least five occasions.

Sleeping rough
Just over half of the purposive sample had slept rough, and almost all of these young people had done so on the first occasion that they ran away (see above). In fact, to some extent, the likelihood of sleeping rough seems to diminish after the first running-away incident, with young people tending to stay with friends or acquaintances, although young people who had initially slept rough often resorted to it on other occasions that they ran away. Thus, there is little evidence of a developing pattern of sleeping rough.

Risky survival strategies

Whilst all of the young people who were away were at risk to a certain extent, we look here specifically at those who resorted to stealing, begging, drug-dealing or survival sex whilst away. Around a third of the purposive sample mentioned using such survival strategies whilst away. By far the most common strategy was stealing, including shoplifting, burglary and car theft. A participant described how he spent his nights 'taking drugs to stay awake for the burglaries' and another described how she survived through:

> *Handouts and going begging* [and how you] *had to watch with the handouts – day centres, if they click on you're under 16 they're quick to call up social services.*

The other three strategies were only mentioned by one or two young people. One interviewee described how she managed to avoid selling sex:

> *Eventually we got picked up by two blokes and we stayed with them. She* [friend] *got involved with one of them. The other tried it on with me. I couldn't handle it so I left there and slept on the beach all night under the pier.*

There was a strong association between these strategies and sleeping rough. All but one of the young people who used risky survival strategies had definitely slept rough. As for sleeping rough, these strategies were usually utilised on the first occasion of running away or very soon after. So, there is little evidence of a developing pattern here either.

Length of time away

As outlined in the previous chapter, there was a wide range of lengths of time for the first running away incident. Young people under the age of 11 seemed more likely to return home without spending a night away. Looking at subsequent running-away incidents, there are some tentative indications here that some young people may develop a pattern of staying away longer, the more times they run away. However, this only seemed to be conclusively the case for around a fifth of the sample. For a larger proportion of young people, the average length of time away seemed to vary or remain much the same as running away progressed.

We identified four young people amongst this sample who had become completely detached from family or substitute care for lengthy periods under the age of 16. Two of these young people had run away regularly, but the other two had only run away a few times and very quickly became detached. All four had had social worker involvement before running away began, and two had been in substitute care. We describe this small group in more detail in Chapter 8.

Travelling outside the local area

Relatively few of the young people (around a fifth) had travelled outside their local area whilst away under the age of 16. Some of these young people had developed this pattern over time, but others had begun from the first time they went away.

Peer associations

There are some notable patterns here, with young people tending to mention more associations with peers at later stages in their running-away experience. However, to a certain extent, this appears to be due to an age effect – i.e. peer associations are more important for teenagers who run away than for younger people, as we saw earlier in the report. Therefore this cannot necessarily be seen as a developing pattern. It does, however, partly explain the fact that older young people seem less likely to sleep rough. More of these young people stayed with friends and acquaintances whilst away, although not necessarily in safe or stable environments (see below).

Dangers whilst away

There was clear evidence of dangers whilst away for around a quarter of the young people. This included being threatened or assaulted on the street, and being involved in drugs or survival sex. However, it was not only those young people who were literally on the street who were at risk. Some young people were sexually or physically assaulted whilst staying with friends, acquaintances or relatives. We have already presented similar evidence from the survey. Thus, whilst the likelihood of such risks seems to increase for those sleeping rough, it must not be assumed that young people who stay with people whilst away are necessarily safe.

Again, there was no evidence that young people were less at

risk on the first occasion when they ran away than on subsequent occasions.

SUMMARY

The evidence presented in this chapter provides a comprehensive and representative picture of young people's experiences of being away. The survey indicates that being away can have some positive aspects for young people. Many young people felt that they had had time to think and relief from pressure whilst away. However, there are also many negative aspects to the experience. Many young people reported feeling lonely, hungry or frightened, and a large minority had faced risks such as sleeping rough and being physically or sexually assaulted whilst away. The majority of young people rely on friends and relatives for support whilst away, but around one in seven relied solely on more risky strategies including stealing, begging and survival sex.

We have also been able to look at the question of whether there is a coherent, consistent or developing pattern in young people's experiences whilst away from home. The research suggest that there is not. There is also no evidence of a difference in running-away experiences according to the age when they happen. However, young people who run away repeatedly do appear to have different experiences (i.e. face more risks) than young people who only run away once or twice. These tendencies are often in evidence from the first time young people run away.

CHAPTER 8

Sub-groups and individual narratives

In this final chapter on running away under the age of 16, we draw together the data discussed in previous chapters and present a number of case studies depicting some identifiable sub-groups of young people who run away or are forced to leave home. These case studies are based on information from one or more young people, but have been modified in some cases where this was necessary in order to preserve individuals' anonymity.

We base our analysis here on both the survey and the interviews with young people. In order to explore the existence of distinct sub-groups, we made use of information on a range of issues, including reasons for running away, background context, behaviour whilst away (including number of episodes, length of time away, where slept, how survived, and so on), involvement with social workers and other agencies, and experience of substitute care.

PATTERNS OF RUNNING AWAY

Stein *et al.* (1994) identified a number of common running-away pathways:

- young people who run away once or twice, usually from the family home, and then stop running away;

- young people who run away from the family, are placed in substitute care and stop running away;

- young people who run away repeatedly, including spending time in substitute care, but who remain relatively attached to the care system;

- young people who become detached, either directly from the family or after going into substitute care.

This model was based on previous research (Newman, 1989; Abrahams and Mungall, 1992; Rees, 1993) and on interviews with a small number of young people who were in contact with projects working with runaways in four cities.

We have been able to develop this model much further with the data collected through the current research project. We will look at four broad running-away patterns and distinguish some common sub-groups within each pattern:

1. Young people who run away once or twice, but who have not spent a night away from home. From the survey, we would estimate that around 6% of the total population of young people have this experience before the age of 16. This amounts to around 43,000 young people per school year.

2. Young people who run away once or twice, including spending one or more nights away from home. From the survey, we would estimate that around 9% of young people fit into this category, amounting to 63,000 young people per school year.

3. Young people who run away repeatedly (three times or more), but do not become detached. From the survey, we would estimate that around 2% of all young people have this experience before the age of 16, numbering around 14,000 young people per school year.

4. Young people who become detached from home and substitute care for six months or more. We are not able to estimate the size of this group of young people as many of them would not have appeared in the survey due to detachment from school. However, the fact that we interviewed 12 young people with this experience out of an interview sample of 200 indicates that their presence is not negligible amongst the population of young people who have run away overnight.

For the first three groups, for whom we do have survey data, we start by briefly comparing a number of aspects of the young people's lives and the nature of their being away (see Table 8.1).

We will refer to specific findings from Table 8.1 throughout this chapter. However, some general points are noteworthy here.

Table 8.1 *Comparison of key home, school and personal indicators by experience of running away*

	Not run away	Run away but not overnight	Run away overnight once or twice	Run away overnight three times or more
Relationships at home				
Expressed one or more negative feelings about relationship with parents	19%	35%	45%	54%
Did not get on with parents	3%	7%	15%	29%
Felt treated differently to siblings	11%	21%	28%	41%
Did not feel understood	7%	15%	23%	36%
Did not feel cared about	1%	3%	5%	16%
Felt parents were too strict	7%	15%	18%	25%
Said parents hit her/him a lot	1%	4%	7%	17%
Experience of substitute care				
Currently living in substitute care	0.3%	1.5%	0.7%	8%
Ever lived in substitute care	2%	5%	6%	19%
Family form				
Both birth parents	72%	59%	51%	47%
Single parent	19%	23%	27%	26%
Parent and step-parent	7%	14%	18%	17%
School experience				
Often truant	3%	5%	10%	20%

Have been excluded from school	9%	19%	27%	41%
Often bullied at school	4%	11%	10%	19%
Personal issues				
Feeling fed up/ depressed	31%	51%	51%	62%
Problems with boy/ girlfriends	16%	30%	32%	39%
Problems with drugs	3%	8%	14%	32%
Problems with alcohol	6%	15%	20%	38%
Getting in trouble with the police	5%	11%	17%	35%
Have friends who have run away	36%	65%	77%	85%

First, there is a substantial difference between young people who have never run away and those who have run away but not spent a night away. The differences between these two groups were statistically significant for all of the indicators presented in the table. Thus, the issue of running away during the day should not be taken lightly. We have not focused on this group of young people in the preceding chapters but will look at some of the issues relevant to them in this chapter.

Second, in most respects, there is also a significant difference between those who have run away overnight and those who have only run away during the day. The exceptions relate to the statistics on parental strictness, depression, problems with boyfriends or girlfriends, and the proportion who currently live in substitute care. For these four indicators, although a visual inspection suggests a difference, the difference is not large enough to be significant. However, note that there was a statistically significant difference according to whether young people had ever lived in substitute care.

Third, in comparing those who have run away once or twice

overnight with those who have run away more often, most of the differences are significant. One notable exception to this is the data on family forms. There was no difference between the two groups in this respect. Further analysis concluded that, whilst young people living in single-parent and step-parent families are more likely to run away, there was no link between family form and the number of times run away. There was also no evidence of differences on parental strictness and problems with boyfriends or girlfriends between those who had run once or twice and those who had done so more often.

We will now go on to look in more detail at each of the four groups of young people listed above who had run away or been forced to leave.

YOUNG PEOPLE WHO RUN AWAY ONCE OR TWICE BUT HAD NOT SPENT A NIGHT AWAY

Elsewhere in the report, for clarity, we have excluded this group of young people from the analysis. However, as Table 8.1 shows, whilst these young people are less likely to have problems in the home, school and personal spheres than young people who run away and are away overnight, they nevertheless have significantly more problems than those young people who do not run away at all.

In general, the triggers that led to these young people running away predominantly related to problems at home (68%). Personal, school and other problems were each mentioned by around a fifth of the young people (23%, 18%, and 17% respectively).

As one might expect, the problems that led to them running away tended in general to be less serious than for those who had run away overnight. Around 18% cited general family problems as the trigger for running away:

Because I had been arguing with my parents and just left. I only ran down the street and to the park but it took my mum 20 minutes to get me home.

The next most common category was young people who needed a break from their situation. Comments such as the following are typical:

*Because everything was getting too much. I needed time to clear
my head and think.*

There was a large number of other reasons for running away, such as
problems at school, conflict with siblings, pressure from parents, and
being in trouble with parents for something. Many of these appeared to
relate to fairly short-lived problems which were subsequently
resolved.

However, there were examples in the survey of more serious problems amongst young people who 'needed a break' or were being
abused at home.

Some of the reasons for needing a break were quite specific:

*Dad recently died and I couldn't cope at home with all the family,
especially my mum and older brother. I didn't want to believe
what had happened.*

Others reflected long-standing problems:

*I had been rowing with my parents for ages and it had become
unbearable. It is better now.*

Not all of the problems had been resolved. One young person aged
15, who had recently run away once, described his situation and experience of being away as follows:

*I hate my life, family and home. Sometimes it's too much to
handle ... I think my life is crap and not worth living ... I was gone
for only one hour before I was found but I was fucking scared.
My dad found me at my friend's house and dragged me home.*

Issues of abuse were less common than for young people who had
run away overnight (see Chapter 4 for statistics) with around 6%
reporting some form of emotional abuse and 5% reporting physical
abuse.

A lot of the emotional abuse related to scapegoating or constant crit-
icism, from the young person's perspective:

*I got fed up with my parents always taking their problems out
on me.*

Because my mum was pure moaning at me for every single little

*thing, and I forgot to take the bins out. She was really
overreacting so I just went.*

Whilst the prevalence of physical abuse and the threat of violence
for this group was not that high, there were indications that for some
young people it was still quite serious:

*Because of being scared of my dad when he gets angry, I think
that he will hurt me. It is not often but we have an argument
nearly every day. He only gets so angry that I have to leave for a
couple of hours once every three months but I feel his temper
needs controlling.*

*Because my real mother was hitting me with the belt and fist so I
had enough and just left.*

The latter young person was now living in foster care: 'Well, they are a
lot better than my real parents'.

In summary then, whilst most of the young people who had only
run away in the day were reacting to relatively minor short-term
problems in their lives which were subsequently resolved, this was
not always the case. It would be wrong to view incidents of running
away for a few hours as necessarily trivial and not worthy of attention. In some cases, this kind of running away is indicative of serious problems in the young person's life with which they may need
support.

YOUNG PEOPLE WHO RUN AWAY ONCE OR TWICE, INCLUDING SPENDING AT LEAST ONE NIGHT AWAY

This group accounts for just over half of the survey sample who had
run away or been forced to leave home. Very little is known about
these young people from previous research and so it is particularly
important to explore the reasons for their running away and their current situations.

As we have seen in Table 8.1, this group have more negative experiences of family life than those who had not run away overnight. However, a slight majority expressed no negative feelings about their
current family relationships.

TRIGGERS FOR RUNNING AWAY

It is interesting to examine the triggers for running away according to current feelings about family relationships. Those young people who currently had no negative feelings about relationships with parents were significantly less likely to cite family and school problems as reasons for running away, although the proportion who cited family problems is still fairly high (63%).

The family problems cited tended to be less severe than for young people who were currently unhappy with their family. For example, the incidence of physical, sexual or emotional abuse as triggers for running away is lower for this group, and the incidence of parental disharmony and less severe conflict between the young person and parents are more common. Nevertheless, there are still instances of young people running away for quite serious reasons (particularly physical abuse) and yet currently not experiencing difficulties with their parents.

RESOLUTION OF PROBLEMS

There appear to be three different patterns here. First, for the majority of young people who fall into this group the problems that caused them to run away were satisfactorily resolved. For example:

I ran away because it was a time my mother and father was splitting up and I felt I couldn't handle the pressure of them arguing, and every time they would argue it would make me feel more upset and lonely because I felt I could not talk to either of them about my problems. I talked to my parents and sorted my head out, then after that things were going fine.

My step-dad was a dick-head and he kicked me out but it's fine now!

I had to leave because I stole my dad's car and got caught smoking weed in my house. I went home and sorted it out with my dad.

Mum finding out that I'm not her little girl anymore. Reading my diary and finding things out the hard way. I went home, mum and dad sorted things out. I now stay out all weekend at my boyfriend's house and during the week we spend a lot of time at my house.

Second, for some young people there was a change in home context which led to the problems receding:

I didn't get on with my dad's girlfriend. I found it difficult and hard to get on with both her and her children. My dad also changed. I knew my mum would let me stay with her as I am very close to my mum. My dad's girlfriend moved out and I went back home.

Third, some young people moved home, either from one parent to the other, to other relatives or into substitute care:

I had to leave because I wanted to move in with my dad and she [mother] *didn't like it so she wouldn't let me in my house. I moved in with my dad into a new house and everything's fine now.*

My mum was pestering me, blaming me for everything, saying I marked her clothes, she was doing this constantly for two years and she always told lies about me. She used to hit me really hard until one day I hit back in about Form 1. By Form 2 she learnt other ways to get at me. It got to the stage when I had to leave. My grandparent looked after me. [I'm] *still there, come home at weekends.*

Although for many of these young people the reasons for running away were relatively minor and were quickly resolved, this was not always the case as we will discuss below.

In summary then, many of the young people who had run away once or twice overnight subsequently resolved the problems which had led to them running away. In most cases within families, this seems to have happened without the intervention of social services or other helping agencies. To a certain extent, it appears that the young person's decision to run away brought matters to a head and facilitated the resolution of the problem.

Young people in this sub-group were relatively unlikely to have ever spent time in substitute care (6%), and almost all were currently living with their family.

However, not all the young people who ran away once or twice had such positive resolutions to their problems. Three groups in particular stand out in the analysis we have carried out.

YOUNG PEOPLE WHO RAN AWAY DUE TO PHYSICAL, SEXUAL OR EMOTIONAL ABUSE

Around 20% of those young people in the survey who had only run away once or twice had done so because of physical, sexual or emotional abuse. Whilst most young people who had run away once or twice were currently happy with their home context, this was less likely to be the case for this group. Three-fifths (60%) expressed negative feelings about their current relationships with their parents or carers, including 41% who felt they were treated differently to siblings, and 22% who said they were hit a lot. This group had a higher than average incidence of sleeping rough (30%) and of being hurt whilst away (20%).

Table 8.2 *Examples of young people who ran away once or twice, and what happened at the end of the incident*

Why the young person ran away	What happened in the end
Because I hate my mum. She always hits me and gives me verbal abuse	*Police found me and took me home*
Dad was drunk and wanted to beat me up because I was behaving badly	*I went home unfortunately*
Because I had problems with my brother, he used to hit me all the time, he was really violent but he doesn't live with me anymore, he lives with my dad now	*I went up dad's then I went home. I told my mum how I felt and things got a lot better. I'm happy with my life at the moment*
Because I was sick of my dad and his girlfriend hitting me.	*My dad said sorry! But he didn't mean it*
My dad kept on beating me up	*I found someone that loved me and went to live with them*
Because I didn't like it at home. My parents were calling me names, e.g. stupid cunt, stupid bastard	*My parents told me if I ran away again they'd kill me, not really kill me, just batter me, but I do get on with them*

They were, however, no more likely than average (for runaways) to have problems at school with truancy or exclusion, although they were more likely than average to be bullied (18%). Similarly, the proportion who had problems with drugs (17%), alcohol (22%) and offending (17%) were not particularly high for runaways.

These young people therefore have comparable levels of family problems and risky runaway behaviour to more repetitive runaways, but lower levels of personal and school problems. Despite having run away for fairly serious reasons, it appears that for a majority of this group, the problems that caused them to run away remain unresolved. Some examples are provided in Table 8.2.

Case Study 1: Anne

Anne entered care with her siblings at an early age due to her mother's inability to cope. After several moves she went to live in a foster home with her brother. She was very close to him and felt a sense of responsibility towards him. Both she and her brother were physically abused by their foster parent over a period of time. Fear of further punishment prevented her from running away:

I couldn't run away from foster care [as my foster parent] *would have whacked me. I sat back once and watched her give my brother two black eyes. Probably if I'd run away from there she would have broke my legs so I couldn't run any more.*

Despite telling her social worker what was happening, nothing was done until her foster parent decided she would have to leave. When the placement broke down she was separated from her brother and given a placement in a children's home. Anger and anxiety at her past abuse, her separation from her brother and the failure of social services to act combined with dislike of her new surroundings. At 14 she ran away for the first and only time:

The only time they did something was when I ran away from the [children's home]. *I just thought to myself, where's my life going? I didn't even like it there so I ran away. Everyone used to run away from there. Nobody likes moving out of places and going to new places, not at the age of 14 when you've moved enough.*

She stayed out all night with others from the unit until she was picked up by the police and returned the next day. She felt the reaction of staff when she returned was initially unsympathetic; that, because running away was commonplace, they failed to explore the unhappiness that underpinned her absence:

You run away and when you go back they don't sympathise with you. They just say to you, 'oh no you shouldn't'. I got grounded for it as well... just because I was unhappy. It were bad, so I didn't do it again.

However, running away did eventually generate some action. She made a planned move to another children's home where she was to settle. She liked the fact that it felt less institutionalised, each child had their own room, and the staff were friendly and supportive. However, looking back she still felt some anger that she had to run away in order to draw attention to her unhappiness:

You shouldn't have to run away from somewhere just to make a young child happy.

Case Study 2: Carlton

Carlton lived with his mother, father and younger brother up to the age of ten. He had suffered repeated sporadic abuse from his father from a young age, and matters came to a head:

One day when I came in from school he just started shouting at me for no reason at all. Then he started to beat the hell out of me ... My mum said that he didn't do it, that I did it myself. How could I do it myself on my back? I had to walk out ... I ran away and stayed at a friend's house.

Carlton stayed away for one night. Then he spoke to his mother and she said that she had asked the father to leave home, so Carlton returned. However, within a year, the father moved back in:

My dad came back. My mum had him back and he was cruel to me. He started drinking and his violence was unbearable. He was violent towards all of us.

Eventually, at the age of 14, Carlton could not cope any more and ran away for the second time:

I couldn't bear his violence, couldn't forgive mum for letting him stay with us. I slept on a park bench with my jacket – no blanket or nothing. I stole food from shops. Sometimes, I went home for food when dad was out.

Carlton was picked up by the police after about a week away, and placed in care, where he remained until he was 16.

YOUNG PEOPLE WHO RAN AWAY DUE TO DEPRESSION AND UNHAPPINESS

Amongst those young people who had run away once or twice overnight, there was a small group of 40 young people whose sole reason for running away was depression or unhappiness:

Because I hated my life and nearly everyone in it. I was so depressed I didn't want to live.

Because I felt very depressed, everything was running back in my mind about the past and I could not handle living in that area where my mother lives.

This small group of young people (constituting around 3% of all those in the survey who had run away overnight), are notable because of the relatively high risks they appear to face whilst away from home. This sub-group had a higher rate of sleeping rough (40%) and a lower rate of sleeping with relatives (10%) than any other group in the survey discussed in this chapter. They also had the highest rate of surviving by risky means (33%) and the second highest rate of being hurt whilst away:

I have nightmares now of being hurt by that man.

This group of young people was more likely (19%) to have spent time in substitute care than other young people who had run once or twice, although relatively few were currently living in care and only one had run away whilst in care.

They were also relatively highly likely to have truanted regularly (26%) and to have been excluded from school (31%).

These young people were less likely than average (amongst the runaway sample) to have problems with drugs, alcohol or offending.

Case Study 3: Sarah

Sarah lived with her mother, father and younger sister. Her parents had a lot of arguments, and as a child Sarah suffered from stress-related symptoms. When she was at primary school, she would pretend to be unwell and would be taken to hospital.

I'm the kind of person who lets the littlest thing get to me. I bottle things up and then I explode at the end of it. I'm a very sensitive person and my mother and father had a lot of arguments through their relationship and they didn't really understand the way I was being affected by the tension. My sister was too young to understand what was going on. I was in hospital nearly all the time, stress-linked problems... I used to make up problems I had wrong with me when I was in primary school and they used to take me to hospital. I did it for affection, for someone to say I was 'here' kind of thing. It was because I thought people were ignoring me.

Sarah was sent to a counsellor and then a psychiatrist:

But because I had bottled so much up over the years, it was difficult for me to express how I felt and sort of where to start. So I just didn't know what to do with myself. I went to see a psychiatrist. I went there for a year and all I did was sit there and look at the clock. The way he was trying to get things out of me was the wrong way of doing it because I was very young.

By the age of 15, she felt she just had to get out of the house:

I had to get out of there. There was so much bad atmosphere in

our house you could cut it with a knife. It was really bad.
I felt better on the move as I could sort my head out. I needed
space to myself. I didn't have any money because I was drink-
ing, I was drinking every day because of the depression. I went
up to sit on the mountain side and stayed out all night. But
another time I took an overdose of Prozac and slit my wrists.
That was when I was with my boyfriend.

Young people who were forced to leave home at ages 14 and 15

Around 60 of the young people who had only been away from home once or twice had been forced to leave home. They were the least likely group (33%) in the survey to be living with both parents, and the most likely (27%) to be living with a parent and step parent.

The key characteristic of this group is that they are forced to leave home by parents either without having ever gone missing previously or in response to their return from their first running-away incident. There was little evidence of physical abuse amongst this group in the survey (only 7% said that they were hit a lot by their parents), but there was a tendency towards unhappy family relationships. Amongst those young people we interviewed who fell into this category, there was often a history of extreme conflict within the family, and in some cases this was compounded by domestic violence or heavy drinking.

Although the survey indicates that these young people were more likely (11%) to have lived in substitute care than the general population of young people, this proportion was lower than for most of the other groups we examine in this chapter.

This group was likely to be away for significantly more lengthy periods than average; almost half (49%) spent a week or more away from home. However, the rate of sleeping rough was very low (5%) and most stayed with relatives (43%) or friends (41%). Despite this, around 12% of this group said they had been physically or sexually assaulted whilst away, suggesting that not all the places they stayed were that safe.

In the purposive interview sample, none of the young people in this category had lived in substitute care before the first running away incident, although some went on to live in care shortly afterwards and all subsequently had social work involvement. However, none had had a social worker for more than a few months before the first incident, and, in the majority of cases, the involvement came as a result of their being forced to leave home. They almost all slept rough on the first occasion that they went missing. Only a minority adopted risky survival strategies whilst away, despite the fact they were sleeping rough.

The fact that in the interview sample most young people in this group had slept rough, whilst in the survey this was relatively rare for this group, is not necessarily contradictory. It is possible that most young people who are forced to leave find support structures to turn to, but that those who do not are highly likely to sleep rough and to go on to develop a pattern of being away.

Case Study 4: Ewan

Ewan lived with his parents who were always arguing, splitting up and then getting together again.

The only memories I have of my mother and father are of them arguing and my mother cooking dinner and chucking it at the wall. They'd get back together and then they'd finish again.

Then Ewan found out his father was beating his mother up.

You see my father was hitting my mother in places where people couldn't see the bruises. When I found out about this and tried to stop him hitting her, my father beat me up and told me to go. Trying to help my mum got me nowhere in the end. He told me to leave. I was 15.

I slept rough. It's horrible. I didn't know what I was going to do, where I was going to stay. You can imagine. You don't know where your next meal is coming from. Sometimes I slept at a mate's house but you know how you can outstay your welcome.

YOUNG PEOPLE WHO RUN AWAY THREE TIMES OR MORE

As shown in Table 8.1, young people who run away three times or more have the highest indicators of unhappiness and problems in various areas of their lives including family, school and personal. Compared to young people who only run away once or twice overnight, this group of young people also have more extreme experiences of being away (see Chapter 7 for details), although, as we have seen above, there are some sub-groups of young people who have only run away once or twice who are particularly at risk whilst away.

Young people who have run away repeatedly have been well represented in previous research, as discussed in Chapter 1. However, the current research gathered data from a far greater number of young people than any earlier study and this has enabled us to explore some issues in more depth than has previously been possible. We have looked in detail at two areas. First, we have examined the initial triggers for running away for this group of young people. Second, we have examined differences in experiences of young people according to the age that they first ran away.

INITIAL TRIGGERS FOR RUNNING AWAY

In our purposive interview sample of 69 young people (see Chapter 2 for further details), there were 52 young people who had first run away before the age of 16, and the findings below relate to those in this group who had run away three or more times.

For the young people interviewed, there were two main triggers for the first incident of running away: family conflict or arguments, and physical abuse. Most of the family conflict was between the young person and her/his parents, but there was also evidence of conflict with other family members. For instance, one interviewee complained that:

> I shared a room with my sister and I had to hoover up her mess.

In some cases, where there had already been a history of violence in the family, the immediate trigger for running away was relatively minor, for example, as quoted above, an argument over household chores; and it was the ongoing nature of the abuse and conflict which was the underlying 'reason' for running away. Conflict was also linked with other issues, such as a parent's mental or physical ill-health, the young person's problems at school, and, for older young people, their widening social networks. For two of the younger children, the trigger for running away on the first occasion was arguments between their parents. One participant who ran away at the age of six due to conflict between parents said:

> *If I stayed out, I wouldn't have to listen to all the arguments; I just like, needed to get out and just clear my mind.*

Physical abuse was a trigger for young people running away for at least a third of the interview sample. The perpetrators of violence included birth parents and step-parents. Usually, the violence was associated with conflict within the family, and emotional abuse (including scapegoating and differential treatment), and parental alcohol problems were also present in some cases. Young people's accounts suggest that this physical abuse was usually ongoing, and there is no evidence of a young person running away due to an isolated incident of violence. Such ongoing abuse as the result of scapegoating was described by an interviewee who lived with mistreatment on a daily basis:

> *Me mam and dad started beating me up every day…I was hit for everybody because I was the eldest at home.*

It seems that young people will endure a considerable amount of violence before running away.

In addition to these two main categories of triggers, two other factors were present for at least five of the young people. First, there was conflict with parents over boundaries. This conflict can be viewed in two ways. In some cases, it appeared that the young people were stretching the boundaries of acceptable and safe behaviour, whilst in others it seems that parents or step-parents were more restrictive than would be considered appropriate for the young person's age. In some cases, both of these tensions were apparent. One interviewee, forced out of home at the age of 14, appears to have pushed the boundaries to the limit by getting drunk and refusing to attend school, but at the same time the penalty of throwing her out appears extreme:

> *I was 14 at the time. I was going in drunk and arguing with everybody all the time. I was kicked out of the house.*

Another research participant who first ran away at the age of 12 described her parents as having unrealistic expectations of her behaviour:

> *They* [parents] *were pressurising me all the time and it hurt me to think why do they want me to be someone else?*

Second, there were a number of young people who were unhappy where they were living, and often ran away in order to go somewhere else where they felt they would prefer to be. This included some young people living in substitute care who returned to parents. One young person described how he used to run away from a children's home:

> *I used to love running away. I was free and could do what I wanted. Butlins was the only place where I could meet girls, get food and a roof over my head and it was fun... I did like being in the home, there were things to do and the staff was funny but some of the rules were doing my head in.*

Other less common triggers for running away included neglect or rejection, differential treatment, not feeling listened to, and parental ill-health.

REPEAT RUNAWAYS WHO BEGAN RUNNING AWAY AGED UNDER 11

The analysis of the interviews and survey suggests that there are some important differences in young people's experiences depending on the age when they first run away, some of which have already been touched upon in earlier chapters.

To recap, young people who first run away before the age of 11 are more likely not to stay out overnight on the first occasion they run away, but, if they do, they seem to be somewhat more likely to sleep rough on this occasion rather than go to friends or relatives. These young people are more likely to experience physical abuse within the family, although not always before the first incident of running away.

In addition, our analysis suggests that they are very likely to run away on a large number of occasions. However, there is not necessarily a developing pattern to the running-away incidents. They may progress to longer more risky episodes of running away, or on the other hand they may develop safer survival strategies over time. They seem perhaps somewhat less likely to adopt risky survival strategies such as offending whilst away than do young people who start running away at an older age.

Compared to older repetitive runaways, this group were more likely to be currently living in a step-family and less likely to be living in a single-parent family.

Our analysis also suggests that this group of young people are highly likely to have social work involvement and that usually this involvement started before they went missing. Presumably, this may be linked to the high incidence of physical abuse amongst this group.

A substantial proportion of this group had lived or currently lived in substitute care. This is backed up by evidence from the survey. Young people who ran away three times or more and first ran away under 11 were the most likely to be currently in residential care (5% compared to 0.3% for all runaways) and the most likely to have lived in care at some point (20% compared to 8% of all runaways).

These young repetitive runaways had a higher incidence of school and personal problems than older repetitive runaways on almost all the indicators listed in Table 8.1. Not all of these differences were statistically significant, but the consistency of the pattern is indicative of a potential difference here.

Thus, young people who start running away before the age of 11 and go on to run away repeatedly represent the biggest challenge in terms of developing effective responses.

The case studies below bring out some of the differences between young people who run away repeatedly according to when they started running away.

Case Study 5: Wayne

Wayne lived with his mother, father, and two brothers until he was five years old when his mum and dad split up. His dad left and took Wayne's two brothers with him. Wayne's mum remarried and he never got on with his step-dad. Wayne was on his own with his mother and step-dad until a new baby arrived when Wayne was eight.

We haven't liked each other since he [step-dad] and mum first met when I was six. He's too strict. He'd never had kids and he would start a row over nothing and he would beat me up.

I told my auntie but she didn't believe me. I was interviewed by the police but nothing came of it. I guess they believed my mum and step-dad over me.

Wayne ran away the first time when he was eight after a beating. He developed a pattern of running away to get away from the arguments and physical abuse. The attention of his mother and step-father were on the new baby. He felt as if they didn't care that he had run away. He would sleep in the park or down by the canal. He was on his own and often felt frightened.

If I stayed out, I wouldn't have to listen to all the arguments and I could get away from being hit. When I returned home, I would get a bollocking and get hit again but I felt they were really glad I was out of the way.

At the age of 11, Wayne ran away to Bristol to look for his dad. He still had friends in the area.

I ran away loads of times. One time I took money [from home] and caught a train to Bristol to look for my dad. I stayed there for two weeks. Mostly I stayed with friends. If anyone asked I said I was staying with my auntie. It was my auntie who came and found me in the end.

Altogether, Wayne ran away about 14 times from the age of eight to 11, until he was allowed to move in with his dad. Going to a new school and falling behind with the work, Wayne felt isolated and truanted a great deal. He got in with what he described as 'the wrong crowd', the only people who would mix with him, and he started using drugs and alcohol. He was eventually excluded from school for starting a fire in the classroom.

When I was excluded from school and got into trouble for car theft and things like that, my dad threw me out. That was when I was 15. I was put into foster care because my mum wouldn't have me back. Foster care was alright. They were the best people I've had. I got my act straightened out there. I found it easy to talk to them.

Wayne's case study continues in Chapter 12, p.154.

Case study 6: Sian

Sian lived with her mother, her father and her younger brother. She has an older brother and sister who already lived away from home. She feels she never got on with her parents and that her brother was always favoured over herself as her father had been in the army and expected that his son would follow in his footsteps. Sian described her father as 'a control freak'. There was a lack of communication between herself and her mother to the point where 'it was difficult to sit in the same room'. At 12/13, Sian got into company of which her father didn't approve because they were going out with boys, drinking and taking drugs. There were big arguments.

The first time she left, it was because she had been out drinking with friends when she was 13. Her father grounded her.

I stormed out the house and didn't go back. I went down the industrial estate and slept in a lorry, a big truck it was, at about 11 at night. I felt frightened. There were noises and it was cold. I went home at three in the afternoon. I'd had nothing to eat. They [parents] just ignored me. After a while we started talking again and started arguing. They just blamed me for everything.

Sian said she had lost count of how many times she had stayed away overnight and that it was 20 or more times between the ages of 13 and 15. Sometimes, she and friends would stay with older lads who had the tenancy of a flat on one of the estates. They would drink cider and use whatever drugs were available. Sometimes, she would just walk around all night. She hated school and truanted 'nearly every day' from the age of 14.

When she was 15, she and a friend stayed away for a week. They stayed with friends and camped out as it was in the summer. She went home after a week and there was a terrible argument and on this occasion her father became violent and threw her out. After that, Sian moved in with her aunt.

I went to live with my auntie. She gave me more freedom than my parents did. It was easier for me.

Sian says that when staying with her auntie, she didn't need to run away any more. About her parents, she said:

They blame me for everything and they think that all the things I have done have affected their lives and they think that only they've got problems. When I see them out now, they just walk past me and don't speak.

Sian's case study continues in Chapter 12, p.155.

YOUNG PEOPLE WHO BECOME DETACHED

The final group that we consider consists of young people who became completely detached, i.e. had no contact with family or substitute care for a continuous period of at least six months before the age of 16. Evidence of some young people being in this situation has already appeared in previous research (Stein *et al.*, 1994).

Of the 200 young people interviewed for the current research, 12 fell into this category. A detailed analysis of these interviews confirmed the findings of the earlier research. We found that the majority of these young people did not run away repeatedly (eight became detached on either the first or second running away incident).

The current analysis also broadens our knowledge about this group, although, of course, findings from a sample of 12 young people are not definitive.

Only three of the young people had experience of living in substitute care before becoming detached, and evidence of social work involvement was only present in one additional case. No other agency interventions were noted before these young people became detached. Thus, the majority of these young people had had no specific interventions with problems in their lives before spending an extended period away from home.

The principal trigger for these young people running away was physical violence. Domestic violence, sexual abuse and peer influence were also in evidence for some of the young people. There was usually a wide background of a troubled life prior to the young person starting to run away.

Not surprisingly, in view of the legal situation, most of these young people adopted risky survival strategies such as offending, drug dealing and survival sex whilst away and most had also slept rough at some point. They also relied heavily on older peers for temporary shelter and support and they also commonly became involved with drugs, often to a serious extent.

Clearly, this is a particularly vulnerable group of young people. The case study on Debbie provides an illustration of some of the features emerging from the above analysis.

Case Study 7: Debbie

Debbie was living with her mother, step-father, brother and two step-sisters. Her step-father treated Debbie and her brother differently from the step-sisters, who were his biological children. He was violent towards Debbie and her brother. She says she used to get into trouble just to get her mother's attention.

I didn't get on with my step-dad. It was because he fetched us up differently from the others. He used to give us real hidings too. I used to be scared to go in the house. And people used to say 'and he's not your real dad anyway' and that would do my head in because my mum would never tell us who our real dad was.

I didn't get on with my step-father. I ran away at 14 away to stay with friends and wouldn't go to school. My mum didn't even bother to look for me. I don't have any contact with her now.

At first, I slept at friends' houses and once I had to sleep in a shed for three nights.

Debbie survived through shoplifting, a 'skill' she had learned before she left home when she had felt that she wasn't getting the things she needed. After a period of staying with friends and sleeping rough, she moved in with a heroin dealer whom she didn't even like. She just had nowhere else to go.

I went and stayed with this lad who was a smack dealer. I didn't know anything about heroin until then. I didn't want to stay with him but I had nowhere else to go and the police were after us. I

> didn't even like him. Then I started taking it because he was taking it. I've been on it for four years now.
>
> I was away all the time from when I was 14. I've lived in seven houses with this lad but we were never settled because he was a dealer.

Debbie phased out her school attendance after she ran away from home at the age of 14:

> I used to go to the teachers and they would give me jobs to do like taking notes. I couldn't do any work. I couldn't concentrate that's why. So I stopped going to school at all. I don't think I was even on the register after a while.

Summary

The research has identified four broad groups of young people who run away: young people who do not run away overnight, those who run away overnight once or twice, those who run away overnight repeatedly, and those who become detached for lengthy periods. Generally, young people face greater risks and problems where either running away becomes repetitive and/or where incidents of being away are very lengthy.

We have identified several specific groups of young people who are at particularly high risk both in their home environments and whilst away. These are young people who run away overnight once or twice due to abuse; young people who run away overnight once or twice due to depression; young people who run away three times or more, especially where the running away started before the age of 11; and young people who become detached for lengthy periods.

However, there is sufficient evidence of cause for concern even for those young people who have only run away for a few hours. The issues faced by young people in all of the groups discussed in this chapter point to the need for a range of interventions.

PART 3

Being away at the age of 16 to 17

CHAPTER 9

Prevalence and characteristics of being away at 16 and 17

For the 16- to 17-year-old age group, the task of estimating the prevalence of being away is difficult. The possibility of surveying a representative sample of this age group is fairly remote, and certainly beyond the resources and timescales of this research project. Studies which have carried out a street census have failed to come up with definitive estimates of young people who are on the streets. Therefore, we decided to gather information from key agencies and professionals, and also to obtain any local research reports in the areas in which we carried out interviews. This method is not wholly satisfactory, and in particular there are definitional issues to surmount. Despite these difficulties, we have been able to build up an overview of evidence and views about prevalence from a wide range of sources. In this chapter, we make use of information from interviews with over 300 professionals and a number of local research reports in 14 areas of the UK.

As stated in the introduction, this research project is not concerned with all youth homelessness in the 16- to 17-year old age group. Many young people who become homeless are accommodated in emergency- and longer-term hostel provision and the needs of this group are outside the scope of this project. We are concerned with young people aged 16 or 17 who spend time away from a stable place to live (whether this is with family, in substitute care, in a hostel, or independent accommodation). This might include young people who are literally 'on the streets' or are sleeping rough, and also young people who have nowhere settled to stay and are moving around from one friend or acquaintance to another.

For this group of young people, unlike the under-16 age group, there seem to be some signficant disparities between types of areas and between different ethnic groups, and we consider the evidence we have gathered under a number of headings below.

RURAL AREAS

We gathered information from agencies and local research reports in four areas with low population density. Three of these areas, Gwynedd in North Wales, Sedgemoor in Somerset, and Strabane in Northern Ireland, would probably fit most people's definition of 'rural'. The fourth area, Mid Sussex, is harder to classify as, although it has a low average population density, there are a number of medium to large towns within it and it is also within close proximity to both Brighton and London.

The general impression from the three clearly rural areas is that there are relatively few incidents of rough sleeping amongst any age group, including 16- to 17-year-olds. A survey undertaken by Gwynedd Council (1998), following up on an earlier Shelter Cymru (1997) study, found that over 45 people had been sleeping rough over a ten week period in Bangor and Caernarfon. Amongst this sample, over half were under 25, although it is not clear how many were under 18. There is therefore some evidence of rough sleeping. On the other hand, several workers in the area felt that rough sleeping was far less common in the area than more hidden forms of unstable homelessness, particularly staying with a succession of friends and relatives. There was also a feeling that young people who were not able to rely on the close-knit community for support tended to move out of the area to cities due to a lack of emergency housing options within the area. There was also some suggestion that rough sleeping might be higher in summer when the tourist season was in full swing and accommodation was at a premium.

The situation in Strabane and Sedgemoor would appear to be very similar, based on the comments of professionals in these areas. One difference was that in Sedgemoor there seemed to be a better stock of emergency housing provision for young people in the area. However, according to the hostels providing this accommodation, this was still not sufficient for the demand, which had increased in recent years.

Given this shortage of accommodation in rural areas, it seems inevitable that young people under 18 who become homeless will have to adopt other strategies: rough sleeping (which seems relatively rare); staying with friends, relatives or acquaintances (which seems more common); or moving out of the area.

In Mid Sussex, despite the different characteristics of the area, the situation seemed similar. One hostel had three emergency beds and a waiting list of 70 young people, more than a third of whom were under the age of 18. These young people were either temporarily staying with friends or in some cases living on the streets.

SUBURBAN AREAS

Two of the three suburban areas, Merthyr in South Wales and Ashfield in Nottinghamshire, from which we interviewed professionals, were industrial areas formerly associated with coal-mining and relatively poor economically.

In common with the rural areas, there were many mentions of hidden homelessness and 'sofa-surfing' in these areas. A number of workers expressed concerns for the welfare of young people in these situations owing to the possibility of their being exploited or caught up in unsafe activities, a point we will return to in Chapter 11. In contrast with the rural areas, however, there was much more evidence of rough sleeping in these areas. In both areas, a recent research study about youth homelessness had identified a significant level of rough sleeping (Wilkinson and Craig, 1998; Hutson and Jones, 1997). The South Wales study of rough sleeping in Rhondda Cynon Taff, an area adjacent to Merthyr and almost identical in character, had found that the level of rough sleeping was comparable to that in large cities and that a significant proportion (43%) of rough sleepers were under the age of 18 (Hutson and Jones, 1997).

The third suburban area, Blackburn, was primarily selected due to the high proportion of young people of Indian/Pakistani/Bangladeshi origin in the area, a group which we will discuss separately later in this chapter. However, those workers making comments about youth homelessness in general identified both hidden homelessness and rough sleeping as common in the area, although there are no figures available.

In these suburban areas, there seemed to be more services geared towards young people and more awareness of homelessness as an issue for under 18-year-olds (including those under 16).

CITIES

We interviewed professionals in seven cities: Belfast, Glasgow, Cardiff, Newcastle, Plymouth, Salford and London. The workers in these areas expressed mixed and often conflicting messages. Some said that there was little or no sleeping rough in the area. However, it became clear that this view may well be due to a lack of awareness since specific city centre outreach services, drop-in centres, and emergency hostels show a different picture.

In most of the cities, at least one of the above kind of agencies reported being aware of significant numbers of young people under the age of 18 sleeping on the streets in the city centre, although often this was temporary and sporadic, being interspersed with periods sleeping staying on friends' floors.

Several research studies confirm this pattern. In Glasgow, a monitoring exercise in 1998 found evidence of at least 83 young people under the age of 18 sleeping rough in the city (Carlin and Bradstreet, 1999). In Salford, researchers (Galvin, Steele and Somerville, undated) found that there were a growing number of young homeless people and that two-thirds of the overall homeless sample of 66 people (not age specific) had slept rough. In Plymouth, a three-week snapshot survey (Gunner *et al.*, 1997) identified 82 young people as homeless, 40% of whom were 16 to 17 years old. A third had slept rough at some time. The study also found that there was a significant incidence of homelessness from surrounding rural areas and that one in five young people had slept rough in the countryside or in the city. In London, Centrepoint (1998) reports that two-fifths of the young people aged 16 to 17 arriving at its central London shelter had slept rough in 1997/8. Data gathering across 14 Centrepoint projects found a link between running away and later rough sleeping incidence. Two-fifths of the young people surveyed in the projects had run away before the age of 16, and over half of these young people (52%) had slept rough compared to 37% of those who had not run away before the age of 16.

Putting together the information from agencies and local research studies, we would conclude that there is probably a significant incidence of young people aged 16 to 17 sleeping rough in large cities in the UK, although this may not be apparent to non-specialist agencies working with young people in general. In addition, many professionals suggested that, as in rural and suburban areas, there was a substantial amount of hidden homelessness.

AFRICAN-CARIBBEAN AND ASIAN YOUNG PEOPLE

The issue of being away amongst African-Caribbean and Asian young people was a specific focus of the interviews with professionals in Lambeth and Blackburn respectively. In addition, information relating to young people from ethnic minority groups was gathered from workers in other areas, particularly Glasgow, Plymouth and Cardiff.

In terms of the prevalence of being away amongst 16- to 17-year-olds, there seems to be a common view for both African-Caribbean and Asian young people. This was that, whilst there is a significant incidence of young people choosing or being forced to leave home amongst these groups, it is less visible than amongst white young people. A number of reasons were suggested for this by professionals.

First, there was a feeling that the streets were a particularly dangerous place to be for African-Caribbean and Asian young people. Traditional street homeless culture was characterised as being white, racist and intolerant. Thus, literally being on the streets may be very much a last resort for black young people.

> The homelessness wasn't an issue in terms of them sleeping out because it was very unsafe for them to sleep out. When we set up a resettlement service and specifically started looking at the needs of black and ethnic minority young people, they started using our resettlement service. So there is definitely a need in terms of homelessness, but you have to target your service differently in order to identify where that need is and [how] best to address the needs of those people.

Second, it was felt that hostels for young people were also often unsuitable places for black young people for several reasons. Both the young people and the staff in these hostels were predominantly white and this made living in them a very isolating experience. Young people often experienced racism if they did move into hostels. In addition, workers felt that many of these were not culturally sensitive to the needs of young people from minority ethnic cultures.

Third, young black people's self-respect meant that they handled things in a different way:

> I think definitely yeh... being black myself. I realise that black people tend to hide their ...all different aspects of their lives, their emotions and what-have-you. If they're going through the same thing as a white person, they tend to hide it you know... mask it in some way... they'll do it in a different way so as not to attract attention. That's what black people are like. And that's why you don't see them on the streets. I'm sure there's loads of them around. But they're just hidden.

It seemed far more likely, then, that African-Caribbean and Asian young people would attempt to utilise support within their communities as far as was practical, rather than resort to sleeping rough or moving into a hostel.

This tendency also means that even workers with a good knowledge of these young people found it hard to estimate the numbers who may be homeless and staying temporarily with friends.

Summary

Although we cannot come up with estimates for the numbers of 16- and 17-year-olds who spend time away from home in unstable situations, the comments of a large number of professionals, and the ease with which we were able to find young people to interview who had experience of these situations, suggests that there is a substantial and often hidden problem. This view is backed up by local research reports which we have gathered.

Whereas, for under-16s, there is little evidence of different rates or characteristics of being away for young people in different kinds of areas or from different cultural backgrounds, for the 16- to 17-year-olds some substantial differences seem to emerge.

In terms of types of areas, there seems to be more sleeping rough in built-up areas than in rural areas, although there may be little difference between suburban areas and cities in this respect. Consequently, in rural areas there may be more hidden homelessness or migration out of the area amongst young people.

Amongst African-Caribbean young people and Asian young people also, most of the incidence of being away seems to be hidden due to fear of racism and lack of appropriate services.

Perhaps the differences between under-16s and 16- to 17-year-olds in the above respects arise because the legal situation for under-16s means that young people who run away need to attempt to remain hidden, whereas for certain groups of 16- to 17-year-olds, particularly white young people in urban areas, the availability of some services means that there is more visible evidence of a problem.

CHAPTER 10

Contexts of running away at 16 and 17

As outlined in the introduction, the legal situation of 16- and 17-year-olds is quite different from that of under-16s in several respects which are relevant to the issue of running away. It is hardly surprising, then, that we found an emphasis on different contextual factors in terms of running away for this older age group. In this chapter, we will look at the context of running away at the ages of 16 and 17, paying particular attention to the factors which are different for this age group, and then consider the triggers that led to young people leaving home.

We will examine the views of professionals (which represent a much more extensive body of data than in relation to the under-16 age group) and the experiences of young people. In terms of the young people, we will make a distinction and draw comparisons between those young people who had run away under the age of 16 and those who had not. Some of the context for the former group has already been presented in Chapters 5 and 6 and is not reproduced here. Out of the purposive sample of 69 young people (see Chapter 2), only 17 had no experience of being away before the age of 16.

THE FAMILY CONTEXT

There was evidence of a substantially different family context for those young people who had first run away after the age of 16, compared to the family context outlined in Chapter 5 for young people under the age of 16. Only three out of the 17 young people in the purposive sample who first ran away at 16 or 17 were living with both birth parents, and the majority had experienced a parental separation. At least seven had also lived with a step-parent at some point in their lives. Although most of these changes in family form happened before the age of 16, repercussions of these events often contributed to the young person running away after the age of 16:

> *They were fighting all the time that I was growing up* [from age 10].

In most of these cases, relationships with step-parents were a major issue for the young person:

> *It was when I started to get older and my step-dad didn't like it. I was starting to wear make-up and short skirts and he didn't like it. And one day, I came in and I had love bites on my neck and that's when it all started and he kicked us out.*

This view was backed up by many of the professionals we spoke to:

> *A big area where we do find a problem is where mum either remarries or gets into a relationship with another bloke. That frequently leads to tension which causes the 16-year-old to feel that they can either no longer live at home or mum to have to make a choice between relationship and the daughter.*

In contrast to the under-16s who had run away, for this older age group the incidence of overt abuse was relatively rare. Only three young people mentioned it as part of their family context in interviews – one case of sexual abuse, one case of physical abuse, and one case of neglect.

On the other hand, a major issue for seven young people was parents' reactions towards their behaviour or lives, with sexuality, drug-related theft and relationships with boyfriends all being sources of conflict between the young person and their parents, which formed the backdrop to the young person running away. In addition, two young people raised issues about over-restrictive parenting. Clashes of perception over what was acceptable behaviour for a young person were usually the root of these tensions, as indicated by one young person who said he was doing:

> *Normal teenage things like drugs, like cannabis. Stuff like that upset my family. They didn't like it so I had to move out. My mum thought I was a bad example* [to younger siblings].

The family context of these young people who run away at older ages is therefore somewhat different to that presented in Chapter 5, with more cases of difficult relationships but less cases of overt abuse.

These findings from the young people's interviews differ from the views of professionals. The workers interviewed identified family breakdown and new family forms as the most common factor, but also put a high emphasis on abuse (both physical and sexual). This is not necessarily contradictory, however, because the professionals were commenting on young people running away at 16 and 17 as a whole, whereas the above analysis makes a distinction between young people in this category on the basis of whether they had or had not run away before the age of 16. The analysis from the young people's interviews (and the survey, for that matter) suggests that, where issues of abuse are present within the family, it is likely that young people will start running away before they reach the age of 16.

Professionals put a strong emphasis also on parents not being able to cope with or control young people's behaviour for this age group:

> *Parenting skills are sometimes virtually non-existent and the child runs wild and then the parent just can't cope.*

This is consonant with the findings from the young people's interviews.

THE SUBSTITUTE CARE CONTEXT

We have already seen in an earlier chapter that a majority of the purposive sample of young people who had run away under the age of 16 had spent some time in substitute care, although this was most commonly after they began running away.

However, for the group of young people who only started running away at 16 or 17, relatively few (four out of 17) had been in care. This is hardly surprising, given the high rate of running away under 16 amongst young people who are in substitute care. Three of these four young people ran away after being returned to their family from care. This suggests that, for young people who have had relatively stable experiences of substitute care and have never run away, the transition to family life at 16 may be problematic and lead to homelessness. The other young person was thrown out of home at 16, placed in foster care and left a week later.

A large number of the professionals interviewed mentioned the importance of care backgrounds as a context to young people running away over the age of 16. Specific concerns voiced by a number of people were perceived inadequate preparation for leaving care, premature age of leaving care and inadequate support after leaving care. As one social worker said:

> Most young people, even if they are at home with both parents [who are very supportive] at sixteen, would not be able to manage on their own. We expect so much more of these young people and they haven't got that safety net. Once they're discharged from the children's homes, they can't actually go back every Sunday and take their bag of dirty laundry and have a nice meal and a bath and someone to say, 'Come on, it's alright, bring your bills and we'll sort those out'.

It was also felt that the tendency for young people who had left care to act as host to other young people could lead to the breakdown of tenancies. On top of these factors, the damaging nature of the substitute care experience, particularly where there had been a lot of movement between placements, was seen as contributing to instability after leaving care. The consequence of these factors was often the breakdown of the leaving care placement, and, as one worker for a nightstop scheme pointed out:

> Usually, there's a planned move on from leaving care, but if that then breaks down we see young people who've come to the end of the line and really haven't got anywhere else to go.

THE PEER CONTEXT

Earlier, we noted the influence of peer relationships on running away for those young people aged 11 to 15, drawing on information from the interviews with both young people and professionals. This issue does not seem to be anywhere near as important for the 16- to 17-year-old age group, especially amongst young people who had not run away under the age of 16. Peer influences were only evident in two out of the 17 interviews with this age group. In addition, peer factors are rarely mentioned by professionals in connection with this age group.

Where they are mentioned, they are usually in connection with relationships with boyfriends/girlfriends and with involvement in drugs. The influence of these on tensions between young people and parents has been noted for a few of the young people in this age group under 'Family context' above.

It seems, therefore, that peer influences leading to running away peak amongst the 11- to 15-year-old age group and then decline for 16- to 17-year-olds.

PERSONAL CONTEXTS

MENTAL HEALTH

A far larger number of workers mentioned mental health problems in connection with homeless 16- and 17-year-olds than in connection with under 16-year-olds. In Plymouth, a local study found that 40% of young people with mental health problems using a drop-in centre also had issues with homelessness (Adams (1996), cited in Gunner *et al.* (1997)):

As the manager of a nightstop scheme said:

I think there is a lot of work that needs to be done around young people and the relationship between mental health and homelessness ... I would say that most, if not all, of the young people who come to us have a level of mental health issues simply by being homeless and going through whatever traumas they've been through to end up in that situation. We are trying to increase our knowledge of the issues because we see it as being very pertinent to our work at the moment.

Specific mental health issues mentioned by workers were depression, self-harm and psychosis.

It should be remembered that there is a disinclination amongst agencies to define young people as having mental health problems and therefore there is some ambiguity over this issue. As one social worker put it:

Here, sensibly, you have to be pretty bad to be taken on by the mental health team and that's right because you don't want to be labelling people when it's not right to be doing that.

As with other issues already discussed, the sample of young people's interviews suggested that, where mental health was an issue, many young people had started running away before the age of 16 and these issues have already been covered in Chapter 6. However, in addition, a third of those young people who had first run away at 16 or 17 reported having mental health issues, predominantly depression.

ALCOHOL AND DRUGS ISSUES

Again, there were many comments about these by professionals. In particular, for this older age group, a few workers talked of an increasing availability of heroin in rural areas. However, it is hard to know how much emphasis to place on the views of a very small number of workers.

Amongst the young people interviewed, drugs and alcohol problems were roughly as common for those who ran away at 16 or 17 as for the young people who had begun running away at a younger age. For most of these young people, these problems had begun before they started running away.

OFFENDING

In contrast with the under-16 group, those who had run away at 16 or 17 rarely mentioned issues with offending. However, bearing in mind that a substantial amount of the offending under 16 was a survival strategy after running away had started, this difference is perhaps indicative of the somewhat wider survival options for the 16- to 17-year-old age group, as well as the kinds of situations which they were in whilst away (see Chapter 11).

Professionals spoke of offending for this older age group largely in terms of a potential source of conflict between young people and parents which could lead to the young person having to leave home.

PREGNANCY AND PARENTHOOD

Professionals made relatively few comments about these issues in connection with young people running away. Our interview sample shows a more mixed picture. There was only one example of a young person running away for the first time due to a pregnancy, but a number of other young women said that a pregnancy had led to their being asked to leave home on a subsequent occasion.

SEXUALITY

A number of professionals cited parents' reactions to young people being gay as a potential trigger for homelessness amongst 16- to 17-year-olds. The purposive interview sample included one young person for whom this was the case.

SPECIAL NEEDS

This was also an issue cited by a small number of professionals, for which we have fairly limited evidence. Again, it applies to one or two of the interview sample.

OVERVIEW OF PERSONAL ISSUES

To conclude this sub-section, we would comment that most of the above issues were only mentioned by a minority of professionals. Each is likely to have relevance for some young people who run away at the ages of 16 and 17, but none seems to be prevalent in the majority of cases. However, when we considered all these issues as a group, we found that the majority of young people who ran away at 16 or 17 had experienced problems in at least one of the above areas before running away.

THE SCHOOL CONTEXT

This is primarily an issue in terms of young people under 16, and we have already covered professionals' views on this in Chapter 6. However, we briefly note here the school experience of those young people who first ran away over the age of 16. In general, whilst many of these young people had had some problems at school, there were lower levels of regular truancy and less occurrence of fixed-term and permanent exclusions than for young people who first ran away at younger ages. Only a third of the older age group could be categorised as having had serious problems at school and only two or three had become detached from the education system before the age of 16.

STRUCTURAL ISSUES

Comments on structural issues for the 16- to 17-year-old age group were very common in the interviews with professionals. There were four key issues here. First, there were difficulties in relation to the changes in housing benefit outlined in the introduction, which can lead to a shortfall in income to cover their rent. A number of professionals felt that this contributed to homelessness for young people. Second, there was the exclusion from benefits of some young people in this age group, again as outlined in the introduction. Third, a number of professionals mentioned the tensions arising in families when young people left school and became a financial burden on their parents. Again, access to benefits is a problem for this group, and the tensions often led to young people being forced to leave home by their parents. Finally, there was the lack of access to local authority housing for this age group. Commonly, local authorities will not give a tenancy to an under 18-year-old unless the young person has a guarantor for the rent.

As one worker from a homelessness project put it, the result of all these problems is:

> A lot of them live from hand to mouth ... They might qualify for some form of benefit but it would be very, very low.

And as the manager of another project said:

> We see a lot of young people living on benefits, those who are entitled to benefits – £29, £36 a week – and trying to live independently on that sort of income is a task that a number of adults with a lot of experience of budgeting wouldn't be able to do, and yet we have the expectation that these young people with very little life experience and life skills should be able to manage.

Additionally, we would note that in Northern Ireland the position of 16-year-olds differs from that in the rest of the UK. Young people of this age are in practice generally not able to access hostel accommodation and this problem was mentioned by a number of the professionals interviewed.

The structural issues mentioned by professionals are evident in around a quarter of the interviews with young people who ran away at age 16 or 17, both as a reason for running away (tensions with parents and overcrowding) or as a difficulty once they had run away.

In general, it seems that issues in relation to benefits and housing policy are particularly difficult for this age group, who are in many ways caught between two systems, neither young enough to access services for children and adolescents, nor old enough to have full adult rights.

COMMUNITY AND CULTURAL ISSUES

The community and cultural issues outlined for under-16s in Chapter 6 are equally relevant to the 16- to 17-year-old age group, and it would be superfluous to reproduce them here. However, one issue which came across strongly from the interviews with professionals about this age group related to the specific tensions between young Asian people (especially women) and their families.

One interviewee commented on the different gender cultural expectations for Muslim Asian boys and girls. For girls, things may be more difficult due to the concept of *'izzat'* (respect), which places an extra burden on them. The interviewee felt that this is also present for Hindu and Sikh young people, but possibly in a more dilute form.

An Asian community worker described the issues as follows:

The girl might feel very repressed in the family atmosphere. In certain family culture or environments, the girls are not seen as fully formed members or fully formed individuals. It's those sorts of issues, which I believe are cultural issues, which cause that. Where the family atmosphere is not very open, it's not very flexible, it's not very welcoming, so in that kind of atmosphere the girls might not see a future ... A lot of the times there is a trigger and something happens within her life and that just makes her think that she has to go. It's not necessarily the family life, that might be okay. The trigger happens, for example, and I've known this because a very close friend of mine ran away. She was a girl where her auntie saw her with a boy, that was the truth, she was happy, but she could not think of going back to her family with the knowledge that they know [that she had a boyfriend] *so she ran away, it's that sort of thing.*

Although there are barriers to Asian young people using general services for young people, as discussed in Chapter 6, some agencies were engaging with this group:

Most of the young Asian people that we've worked with have left because of disputes about boyfriends and girlfriends and parents not approving, especially not approving if they are not an Asian boyfriend or girlfriend, about young people becoming pregnant or girlfriend gets pregnant and it's seen as very shameful. Also those kind of things are more cultural problems really and I know that the young people in Blackburn now who are Asian who perhaps kick against the culture a little bit, that is definitely the main reason why we get young Asian people coming [here]. *And we have a high success rate of them going home, definitely.*

AGENCY INTERVENTIONS

There was evidence of a wider range of agency interventions for young people in this age group, including statutory workers and a variety of non-statutory agencies. Most young people at this age were in contact with at least one agency.

STATUTORY AGENCIES

Young people's experience of social workers and probation workers at age 16 and 17 seemed relatively positive:

He [social worker] *is excellent. He got me out of hospital in two week. I'd been there three month and I was homeless for a month so that's why they kept me in there so I wasn't on the streets; the social worker wouldn't have me on the streets.*

They [the probation service] *have got me in here* [hostel] *and stopped me going to jail.*

COUNSELLOR

Five of the young people in this age group were currently receiving counselling, and this was generally received positively:

They don't tell you what to do with your life; they advise you and help you to open up and you know everything is confidential ... they've got a way of opening you up ... you just tell the truth and spill out all your problems. It does help a lot.

DROP-IN CENTRES

Drop-in centres were the most commonly mentioned agencies by young people in this age group, and mostly their view of these services was positive:

It's open in the evenings and you can come here. If you need to talk to someone you can.

Everyone's friendly, they'll give you advice, and you can see counsellors and whatever else you need. My self-confidence went up a lot as soon as I started coming in here.

I don't think they were very good 'cos they just gave me this list of places to call for flats and I don't like talking on the phone.

I actually quite enjoy it, but my friends are against mixing with protestants – but why not – protestant is the same person as me – I don't believe in religion at all.

TRIGGERS FOR BEING AWAY

Having considered the context in which being away at the age of 16 and 17 takes place, we end this chapter with an examination of the triggers that led to young people choosing or being forced to leave home.

There was a total of 74 incidents of being away at 16 and 17 years of age amongst the purposive sample.

The most common trigger for being away was conflict at home, which was the principal reason for 27 of the young people. The other key identifiable reasons were abuse (seven young people), unhappiness at home (seven young people) and pressure to leave from outside the household (five young people).

Around half the sample were forced to leave on at least one occasion at 16 or 17, confirming the pattern already observed earlier in the report for this phenomenon to increase with age.

COMPARISON OF TRIGGERS ACCORDING TO AGE

Earlier in this chapter, we described the family context of the young people who first went missing at 16 or 17. These young people usually lived in disrupted or reconstituted families, there was less evidence of overt abuse than for young people who ran away or were forced to leave before the age of 16, and there was an increased level of conflict over the young person's behaviour. Relatively few young people in this older age group had any experience of living in substitute care.

Not surprisingly, this context is reflected in the triggers for young people being away, which were identifiable for 16 of the 17 young people who first spent time away at 16 or 17. The sample divides broadly into two groups: those who chose to leave and those who were forced to leave. All of these young people were living with their family before the first incident of running away.

Seven young people chose to leave. For three of these young people, all female, the triggers for leaving were linked to abusive family environments – one instance of sexual abuse, one instance of physical abuse, and one instance of having witnessed a long pattern of domestic violence. For the first two of these cases, the young people also experienced their parents as over-restrictive. For the other four, the main trigger was family conflict or very poor quality of relationships, including arguments over boyfriends and not having a job.

> *I met this man who was 24. He was on smack and my mum didn't like it. Then she found out I was pregnant and wouldn't get rid of it and the rows started and I moved out.*

Nine young people were forced to leave by parents. There was no apparent history of physical or sexual abuse amongst this group, although one young person had been neglected. The triggers for being thrown out were primarily arguments linked to parents' disapproval of the young person's behaviour (including being pregnant, having a boyfriend, offending, getting involved in drugs and stealing from parents).

In the other cases, there was evidence of declining relationships which sometimes included conflict linked to economic stresses where the young person had left school and did not have an income.

> *I'd have put up with it but it were getting to the stage where we couldn't even be in the same room. So in the end he just kicked me out.*

The triggers for running away appear to be substantially different with less overt abuse and more disharmony for the over-16 group. There is also an increasing incidence of young people being forced to leave home.

Thus, we can tentatively suggest that perhaps the key difference between those who first ran away at 16 or 17 and those who first ran away before is in terms of the relative prevalence of young people being thrown out due to family conflict, and those who chose to leave abusive contexts, with the former pattern appearing to be more common amongst the older age group. This observation fits in with the views of many professionals interviewed, who commented on the increased tendency for parents to eject young people once they had reached the age of 16. For example, a housing officer reported that:

> Parents say, 'It's not my responsibility any more, she's sixteen, she's moved out and she can't come back and we want no more to do with her'.

Summary

The family context of young people who first spent time away at 16 or 17 differed from those who had run away under 16, with less evidence of overt abuse and more evidence of family conflict and breakdown, often leading to young people being forced to leave home.

Some contextual issues which were important for the under-16 age group had less signficance for this older group. Relatively few of the young people who had not run away before the age of 16 had spent any time in substitute care, a history of serious problems at school was less common, and the significance of peer relationships as a contributory factor to leaving home was less pronounced.

Issues relating to mental health, alcohol, and drugs were as prevalent amongst young people who first left home at 16 or 17 as those who had run away at a younger age, although offending was perhaps less of an issue.

Economic factors were more important for this age group. The impact of current benefits policies relating to 16- and 17-year-olds seems to be an important contributory factor for some young people in this age group being forced to leave home.

CHAPTER 11

Experiences of being away at 16 and 17

In this chapter, we will explore the experience of being away from a stable place to live at 16 and 17. All in all, we consider the experiences of 48 young people – 11 who had first run away before the age of 11, 20 who had first run away or been forced to leave between the ages of 11 and 15, and 17 who had spent time away at 16 to 17 years of age.

In reading the findings, it is important to be aware that we have not sought to provide an overall picture of young people leaving home and becoming 'homeless' at 16 or 17. The young people we spoke to were specifically selected due to their having some experience of running away *and* being in unstable situations. There will be many other young people who leave home and find stable accommodation (a partner, other relatives, a hostel or a flat) without having these experiences. Thus, whilst for the under-16s we have described a representative picture based on a large survey as well as almost 200 interviews, here we are looking at the experiences of a specific sub-sample of young people.

LENGTHS OF TIME AWAY

It is not easy to establish the length of absence on the first occasion for some of the interviewees. However, where we were able to be clear about this, it seemed that young people were away for longer periods than for under-16s, with the minimum being one week. Some young people never returned home after the first incident of being away at 16 or 17.

LEVELS OF DETACHMENT

Despite the conflicts which had often given rise to young people running away, only seven young people were completely detached from their family during this period, although for a further 11 there was a repetitive pattern of turning to family for support, sometimes including a return home, only for the relationship to break down again. It is notable, for example, that all the young people who returned to their family after first being away at 16 or 17 soon left again, usually because the issues that led them to leave the first time recurred or worsened. For example, one young woman who had suffered physical abuse for many years described how she realised things were never going to change:

> It changed for a day or two, everyone tiptoed around me. Then everything went back to the same. No matter how many times they say sorry, they'll always do it again. I realised this isn't for me, it's bound to be wrong. I've had to run away twice. Something isn't right. I realised this house isn't for me. It didn't change the first time, so why should it change the second time? So I didn't go back.

Sources of support

All of the young people were receiving support from others during the periods when they were away. In most cases, this involved a mixture of informal support from friends and family and formal support from agencies. There was substantial evidence that these young people had access to a much wider range of services than under 16-year-olds who run away. This included the possibility of independent supported accommodation in hostels and housing projects – an option which is only exceptionally open to young people under the age of 16 for the legal reasons outlined in the introduction. Additionally, there seemed to be a wider use of advice, drop-in and information services than for the under-16 age group. A likely explanation for this is that young people who run away at 16 and 17 are rarely returned home by the police and therefore are much freer to approach agencies for support. Young people in this age group often commented positively on the support they had received from both statutory and non-statutory services, including advice and counselling agencies run by national and local non-statutory organisations:

In Blackpool, I went to a drop-in day centre. There we could have a game of pool, toast, coffee, biscuits, food. The soup run was good. They were nice people to go out of their way to help people like I was. They used to talk to us and were friendly.

WHERE THE YOUNG PEOPLE SLEPT

Over a third of the young people slept rough at some point whilst away, even though there were wider emergency accommodation options for this age group. However, one should bear in mind that we targeted young people who had spent time away from a stable place to live, so it is hardly surprising that some slept rough and is not necessarily representative of all young people who leave home at 16 or 17.

GEOGRAPHICAL MOBILITY

In general, young people were more geographically mobile in this age group. Twenty-one young people moved out of their local area, some travelling hundreds of miles (e.g. Glasgow to London and then to Cardiff). At the time of the interview, nine of these young people were still living away from their area, whilst 12 had returned to it.

SURVIVAL STRATEGIES

In addition to the possibility of agency support, young people aged 16 and 17 are to a limited extent more able to access legitimate financial support through work or claiming benefits. Nevertheless, there was still evidence of a heavy reliance on other survival strategies. At least 15 of the young people were dependent on friends or relatives whilst they were away, and a further 14 survived through illegal activities (stealing, begging, etc.). As for the under-16 age group, we found very limited evidence of them using sex as a means of survival, although it is always possible that this was a strategy young people were reluctant to disclose.

RISKS

As with the younger age group, there was considerable evidence of the risk involved in running away. Three young people were physically assaulted whilst away, another was harassed by older people on the streets and a further two spoke of their fears of being attacked:

I got hassled sometimes by druggies and old tramps and that. I just said to go away. It was not easy to relax – you have to keep an eye on other people when you're sleeping rough – always look over your shoulders or through the corner of your eyes.

Also in common with the younger group, whilst sleeping rough appeared the most risky strategy, young people staying with friends were not necessarily risk-free as two of the physical assaults occurred in this context – one where the young person had had to move with her baby to the house of a female friend.

Three days after she was born, I moved to [friend's name]. *Her boyfriend,* [name], *hit me. He spat in my face and slapped me across the face. He kicked me and he was calling me everything.* [Friend] *did a statement – he keeps hitting her too … It was scary there.*

In addition to this overt evidence of danger, reliance on drugs and alcohol to cope whilst away was evident for some of the young people, and a number described feeling cold whilst sleeping rough and missing their family, including one young woman who said:

I slept under a bridge and in the park. It was a really bad experience. I was freezing. I was starving. All I wanted was to go to a nice loving home.

In stark contrast, one young person felt that the experience had been broadly positive, having enjoyed the freedom of three years mostly on the road:

I was very happy travelling … Getting my independence [was] *one of the best things. I had a pretty good life. I was on the go all the time. I used to get up in the morning and look at the map and see Preston and that's it, I was off to Preston!*

There was some evidence of differences between those who chose to leave and those who were forced to leave, with more of the former group sleeping rough and consequently using illegal survival strategies.

PROBLEMS WITH DRUGS AND OFFENDING

Issues related to drugs and offending were, in general, very prevalent amongst this group of young people. At least 22 young people used or sold drugs and at least 21 committed criminal offences.

HOW THE INCIDENTS ENDED

Of the young people who first left home at this age, six of the young people returned to the place they had left (family); five went to live temporarily with a sibling, girlfriend/boyfriend, or friend; four moved into other kinds of accommodation (hostel, mother and baby unit, or bed and breakfast); and one (the last quoted above) remained homeless for three years until returning home when his father died. Thus, for most of the young people, the first incident was resolved fairly positively, although this resolution was often only temporary.

Eventually, most of the 48 young people in the sample left home permanently. At the time of the interview, just over half (25) of the young people were living in a hostel. Of the remainder, seven were living in their own independent accommodation, three with family, three with friends, three in substitute care, two with a boyfriend, and one in a night shelter. The remaining four young people were in unstable or unclear situations.

COMPARISON WITH THE UNDER-16 AGE GROUP

It is interesting to compare experiences of being away at 16 or 17 with those of young people away under the age of 16. There are both similarities and contrasts between experiences of being away under and over the age of 16.

Similarities included where young people slept, how they survived, and the risks that they faced whilst away. There were similar levels of sleeping rough, with around half of both age groups having resorted to this at some point. There was also evidence of similar risky survival strategies, despite the increased possibility of some young people in the 16 to 17 age group having the means to support themselves through work, savings or benefits.

The key differences relate to lengths of time away, geographical mobility and the options the young person had open to her or him. To the extent that we were able to ascertain lengths of time away, these seem to be considerably longer for those young people over 16. Young people in this older age group also seemed to be more geographically mobile than under 16-year-olds. Moreover, there was evidence of young people at 16 and 17 having more options due to their different legal situation. Some were able to claim benefits to support themselves whilst away from home, and there were more emergency and longer-term accommodation options available for this age group.

SUMMARY

This chapter has looked at the experience of young people who spend time away from a stable place to live at the ages of 16 and 17, based on 48 interviews with young people.

There is evidence of young people spending significant amounts of time in unstable situations, in some cases never returning home. Whilst the majority of those interviewed had eventually found a stable place to live, this was often not a simple process. Many of the interviews illustrate the vulnerability of young people who are away from home at this age. Over a third of the young people slept rough, and a similar proportion relied on risky survival strategies such as begging or stealing in order to survive. Young people who depended on friends or acquaintances for support could also find themselves in vulnerable situations.

CHAPTER 12

Sub-groups at 16 and 17

I n this chapter, we look at sub-groups of young people who are away from home at 16 and 17 years of age. We make use of case studies, as we did in Chapter 8.

Our analysis suggests that there were some important differences in several aspects of running-away patterns at 16 or 17 for young people who first ran away at different ages. Whilst we do not have a representative sample here, we have employed statistical tests to ensure that the differences we note have met the usually acceptable standards of significance (here, we use a confidence level of 95%).

Young people who first ran away before the age of 11 and were still running away after the age of 16 appeared to be much the most likely to travel outside the area. Nine out of 11 young people had done so, and this pattern seems less prevalent as the age of the first running-away incident increases. None of the young people who first ran away at 16 or 17 had yet permanently moved out of their local area, although six had spent some time away and then returned.

Fitting in with this pattern, there were also higher levels of detachment from family for those young people who had first run away at a young age. The majority of these young people were now completely detached from their family, whilst two-thirds of those who had first run away at 16 or 17 were still relatively attached.

Partly as a result of the above tendencies, those young people who first ran away young were more likely to be reliant solely on formal support from agencies, whilst generally, the young people who had started running away from the age of 11 onwards also had informal sources of support through either friends or family.

The above differences were statistically significant. At face value, there appeared to be higher levels of drug usage and offending amongst the young people who had first run away before the age of 16. Similarly, there appeared to be some tendency for the these young people to be more reliant on illegal means of survival. However, these differences did not meet the criteria for statistical significance.

Based on those differences which were significant, however, we can say with some confidence that young people who start running away at a younger age show, by the age of 16, higher levels of detachment and mobility than those who start running away at a later stage.

In order to illustrate the points coming out of the above analysis, we provide four case studies. Two of these (Wayne and Sian) are continuations of case studies presented in Chapter 8, relating to young people under the age of 16. The other two (Sandeep and Sinead) are new case studies, illustrating some of the patterns of being away for young people who had not run away under the age of 16.

Wayne's story is illustrative of some of the tendencies highlighted in the above analysis. Wayne first ran away at the age of 8, and went on to run away more than ten times. He was thrown out of home at 15 and placed in foster care (see Chapter 8 for further details). Wayne's experience at 16 reflects some of the common themes for young people who run away repeatedly from a young age: a lack of family support networks, geographical mobility, and a reliance on agencies for support.

Case Study 5: Wayne at 16 plus (*continued from p.119*)

Because the foster placement had been successful, it was thought it would be a good idea for Wayne to progress to living in independent accommodation. This did not work out too well as he was inundated by friends and acquaintances who had nowhere to go. There was a lot of drug taking going on and some of the friends were sleeping on the floor. Wayne got into debt over his drug use. He was also in arrears with his rent. These debts made Wayne decide to leave the area. He 'jumped' a train to Cardiff.

When I got to Cardiff, I used to sleep around on the streets like. I used to sleep in bus shelters, in an arcade by the steps. I was woken up a couple of times by the police because I was in the way of the cleaners. I slept wherever I could really, sometimes in the car parks. Once I got to know some people, I was sleeping with a couple of people. I felt a lot safer then.

The people he hung around with on the streets were of a mixed age group. These people all looked out for one another. He went to the *Big Issue* for help.

That was when I started selling the Big Issue. *They badged me up straight away and that's when I started making some money then so I could feed myself.*

Wayne is living in a hostel at present and is still selling the *Big Issue*. Wayne feels that he is beginning to get on his feet again and hopes to get a council flat in the near future.

Sian first ran away at the age of 13 due to deteriorating relationships at home, and after running away numerous times she went to live with an aunt. In contrast to Wayne, Sian maintained some links with her family, remained in her local area, and also had a close network of friends on which to rely.

Case Study 6: Sian at 16 plus (continued from p.121)
At 16, Sian became pregnant. She and her boyfriend split up. She lives in an area with a high level of empty properties and the local authority was able to offer her the tenancy of a flat. Sian found living on her own a traumatic experience. The council flat she lived in was broken into a number of times. Her door was kicked down on four occasions. She became depressed and unable to sleep. She attributes the miscarriage she suffered to the upset she experienced.

I'm staying round friends' houses at the moment. Quite a few friends really. It been like this for two months now. I had a flat. I had a lot of trouble up there because I was young and living on my own. I had a lot of break-ins and my nerves were so bad I had to get out. So I've just been staying around here.

Sian is glad to be away from the flat, but she says:

It's hard having nowhere to live, nowhere to have a long bath or cook a nice meal.'

Sian sees a counsellor weekly and is taking Prozac. She gets some support from her aunt and she is on a housing association waiting list. She hopes to be housed in more suitable accommodation in the future.

The final two case studies illustrate some of the common features amongst young people who first leave home at the age of 16 and 17. These include in Sandeep's case being forced to leave and having problems with drugs, and in Sinead's case the build-up of pressure once she reached the age of 16 and a reliance on family support networks.

Case Study 8: Sandeep

Sandeep lived with his father, mother and younger sister. They moved from Scotland to London. He had problems at school: truanting, getting suspended and finally expelled. This was largely to do with drug use. He started stealing from his parents and they threw him out when he was 16. He slept rough for a month. He slept in parks – 'anywhere'.

I didn't know of anywhere to go. I was coming off crack cocaine and I wasn't thinking straight. I got jumped, had fights, was beaten up and robbed while I was sleeping. It was depressing. I had suicidal thoughts. I knew I had screwed myself up.

He survived by shoplifting, begging and went to soup kitchens and day centres. After a month, he went to a cold weather shelter and later on to a hostel. He has never returned home.

I was kicked out once and I have never returned because they told me not to. I don't speak to them anymore.

Sandeep is regretful. He feels that things might have been different had he been able to live in a different area and had a different choice of friends. He says:

I now realise who my friends are and where I screwed up.

Case Study 9: Sinead

Sinead lived with her mother and father until they split up when she was six years old. She lived in various places with her father until she was 14, when she moved in with her mother in Belfast. At 16, her mother threw her out. Sinead's mother has a night job and Sinead was expected to look after her young sister and brother.

She goes to work at seven in the evening and returns at seven the next morning. I've always complained about it because I could never see my friends or do my school work.

One weekend, she trailed the quilt off me and told me to get out of bed. She's always like that, in moods. I thought nothing of it. When I was in the kitchen, she told me she'll quicken me up and took a black bin bag and put all my stuff into it. She told me to go.

Sinead left without any possessions or money and did not know where to go.

I walked around for a bit but I'd no money. I was going to go to my granny's but my mum said she interfered too much so I didn't go there. I went to my cousins' house but they weren't in. I saw my aunt and she lent me 50p to go down to my mate's house. I spent the first few nights at my mate's house, then stayed at my granda's house, then I moved into hostels. I was used to it because I had always been passed around different places. I was never settled anywhere.

I knew she [mum] was going to throw me out some day because the same thing happened to my big sisters when they were 16 or 17. It was still unexpected. Now she keeps threatening to my brother and sister that they are the next to go.

SUMMARY

In this chapter, we have identified differences in experiences and patterns of being away at 16 and 17, depending on the age when the young person first ran away or was forced to leave home. There are some aspects of being away which vary little across the different sub-groups. However, young people who first ran away at a younger age were more detached at this age than young people who first ran away at an older age. This finding points to the long-term effects of running away under 16 on young people's lives and suggests the possibility that young people with extensive experience of running away at a young age are likely to remain a marginalised group as they move into adulthood.

PART 4

Discussion and conclusion

CHAPTER 13

What could have been different?

In this chapter, we summarise the views of young people and professionals about what could be done to prevent young people from running away or having to leave home, and what could be done to help young people who are away from home.

The views of young people were gathered systematically through the interviews which concluded with a number of questions about how young people felt they could have been helped and what they felt should be done in the future to help young people in similar situations.

The views of professionals were gathered through questions about gaps in services for the young people with whom the research is concerned.

YOUNG PEOPLE'S VIEWS

We will look at young people's responses under three categories:

• preventative work;

• help for young people who are away under 16;

• help for young people who are away at 16 or 17.

However, one type of response cuts across this categorisation, that is the need for more accessible information about services that are available to help young people, which was mentioned by over 30 of the interviewees. Many said that they wished they had been more aware of places they could have gone for help:

> *I didn't know at first that help existed. You need advertising to let young people know what's available.*

It is also important to note that some young people felt that nothing could have prevented them from running away, and others acknowledged that, even if help had been offered, they would have refused it. This was especially the case where running away was linked to peers, and drug/alcohol use, although, in retrospect, some of these young people recognised that ignoring the advice of adults was the wrong thing to have done.

Also, with reference to helping those already on the run, perhaps especially the under-16s, it should be said that there was often a strong feeling of confusion, of an inability to think about anything other than the immediate problem of survival. There was no mental space to consider the underlying problems. For example, one young person said he just wanted:

> *Someone to guide me, someone to pull my strings, to tell me what to do.*

Another explained:

> *Some people feel more secure running away. I felt as if I was inside a building with four walls, a shut window, a shut door. I felt someone was going to come along and kill me. If I was outside, I had no walls, no doors. I had four ways I could escape and I could run in any direction.*

PREVENTION

The suggestions listed below about preventing running away and being forced to leave applied to all young people under the age of 18. We consider here, in order of the number of mentions, all ideas suggested by more than one young person.

Family support/mediation services

> *Some sort of counselling – maybe where families can go and sort stuff out and stop arguing.*

Over 50 young people felt that family support and mediation services would be helpful to prevent young people from running away or being forced to leave. These services might:

- support parents with mental health, substance abuse or divorce/separation problems, which might reduce tension/arguments;

- help to prevent family break-up and/or entry to care;

- improve communication within families, possibly acting as advocate for young person as/when necessary;

- where problems are not amenable to mediation, at least help to plan next steps in a more coherent way.

Many young people were extremely critical of their parents' ability to look after, love and care for them, which also suggests a potential need for the development of better parenting skills.

Advice/counselling services for young people
Twenty young people felt that advice and counselling services could help prevent young people from running away. They could provide opportunities to talk/be listened to and approaches that could draw young people out. Confidentiality was a key issue here, and some young people recognised they had been very reluctant to disclose their problems:

> *I didn't really talk to people, so they didn't know what was wrong. I thought then, it's none of their business. I'll deal with it my own way. But that's the wrong thing to do.*

School-based services
School-based services were mentioned by 16 young people. Ideas included:

- awareness-raising on a wide range of issues as part of the school curriculum, including making use of outside speakers, role plays and so on. Some young people suggested that this would be better offered by outsiders, as there might be a reluctance to believe teachers;

- peer support, making use of older young people who had been through experiences, as these young people would have a great deal of credibility;

- a confidential counselling service attached to schools: it was felt that young people would be more likely to open up about abuse, bullying etc., if they were patiently talked to over time;

- the need for teachers to be especially vigilant over and sensitive to emotional difficulties that their students are facing.

Intensive help with substance-misuse issues
Thirteen young people mentioned the need for early help to prevent young people developing serious drinking or drugs habits at a young age.

Trusting/believing young people
A general point mentioned by 13 young people was the need for all adults – parents and professionals – to respect and believe young people when they talk about their problems and to act on what they are told. Many young people felt undermined by experiences of not being believed, especially over allegations of abuse:

> *If my mum was to sit and talk to me and believe me more often. They take the teachers word over me.*

Improved social services response
Twelve young people suggested ways in which they felt social workers could have helped them more effectively. These included social workers:

- being more available, more directly supportive and more sensitive about family situations;

- offering more advice and support to young people about other sources of help;

- being better at planning an ordered move into substitute care if needed.

Improvements to the care system
Eight young people mentioned specific improvements to the care system:

- tackling peer pressure and bullying;

- more stable/settled placements for those in care;

- the need for young people to have time and space to talk and think about their problems and future in a 'natural' way;

- talks by groups of young people who have been in care and had running-away experiences, as 'peer deterrent talks';

• peer support groups for young people in foster care;

• more help with leaving care.

Day/evening centres and activity centres

A few young people suggested that 18-hour-a-day youth club type provision could alleviate a lot of the boredom, peer pressure, and so on that leads to trouble and danger on the streets.

Anger management

Three of the male interviewees talked about how it would have helped if they had been taught useful strategies for dealing with their tempers, which they readily acknowledged could often get beyond control.

RESPONDING TO YOUNG PEOPLE WHO RUN AWAY OR ARE FORCED TO LEAVE UNDER THE AGE OF 16

Safe houses for under-16s

The most common need identified for under-16s who are away from home was more accessible emergency accommodation, which was mentioned by over 50 young people. It was felt that this provision should be on a small, homely scale. It could provide a safe space to collect thoughts, staff who listen carefully and do not judge, and could possibly have a mediation service attached to negotiate with the family. Many young people suggested that it was important that someone could phone home on their behalf to reassure parents that they were safe.

Young people felt that short-term accommodation of this kind would be a better option than going immediately into substitute care.

Some young people felt that it was very important that staff should have first-hand experience of the types of issues that young people were facing – not just be trained in theory.

Advice/support centres

The next most commonly mentioned (over 25 mentions) need was for advice and support centres, including day centre/drop-in facilities, offering useful information plus the chance to talk with a counsellor if necessary, and practical support. These would be places where people could go during the day, where they could be usefully occupied and not be in danger. As with the above suggestion, there were mentions again of the need for such services to have staff who have first-hand experience of running away/homelessness.

There was also a suggestion of a Childline-type service, but with the ability to refer directly to usable services for those on the streets.

Family mediation

Family mediation services were mentioned by ten people as a potentially useful service for young people who are away from home. They could offer a neutral setting where a young person could perhaps meet with someone they trusted – a friend or a family member – with an advocate present, as a first stage in contact with the family. This kind of service could help to resolve family problems and negotiate a return home.

A more sensitive approach from the police

Five young people felt there was a need for police officers to adopt a more caring, supportive response to vulnerable young people they pick up from the streets.

> *Young people under 16 should not be feeling frightened of police and social services. Running away should not be seen as a crime. Young people should be given a safe space and reassured to contact police and social services for help. They should not be in fear of getting caught and taken back home. The information put out to young people through schools should make it clear that those who run away usually do it through no fault of their own and because they are under stress, and that there are services to help and look after them until they can sort things out for themselves – young people should be given the chance to decide for themselves. At the moment, it is like you have committed a crime and they would be sending out the police to find you.*

Street services

Four young people mentioned the need for outreach workers on the streets to engage with young people who are living rough and provide 'no strings' advice and information and to offer accommodation as appropriate.

Longer-term accommodation
Four young people felt that there ought to be longer-term semi-supported housing for under-16s to house those who cannot return home from a hostel.

Income
Four young people felt that, in special cases, under-16s should be able to access some sort of welfare benefit.

RESPONDING TO YOUNG PEOPLE WHO ARE AWAY AT AGE *16* AND *17*

Some of the most common suggestions presented in this section, e.g. accommodation and advice services, relating to 16- and 17-year-olds were similar to those for the younger age group. However, different needs were also identified for this age group.

Supported hostels
Over thirty young people mentioned the need for more supported hostels. Particular comments were made about the shortage of places in some particular areas, and also the need for these services to provide a period of stability and security and to help young people prepare for independence.

Advice/support services
A similar number of young people pinpointed the need for more advice and support services:

> If you are 16 and have lived with your parents all your life, you've been wrapped in cotton wool all your life. Your parents are there to protect you. Then, if you're straight into the big bad world, there should be support, help and advice, for these young people. Help for accommodation, money, help you budget etc. Stuff you've never had to do while you're living with your parents.

The importance of these services being 'young-person centred' was emphasised. Young people need to be listened to and believed. There was a suggestion that utilising peer support from ex-users would be effective.

A particular gap was identified in terms of generic counselling services for young adults:

> *There are things for people with drugs problems, but nothing for young people who just want to talk to someone for help when they are down.*

Street services

Ten young people mentioned the need for practical support whilst on the streets, including access to blankets, clothes, food, advice, and support. Some of these young people pointed to others they knew who were condemned to the streets as they were banned from hostels.

Income

Eight young people mentioned issues to do with benefits. There was a call for a restoration of benefits to those who are 16 or 17, which would reduce the pressure to engage in crime and use sex as a means of survival. Delays in calculating and receiving benefits were also mentioned as problems that needed to be resolved.

Housing issues

Three young people suggested that local authority housing could be better utilised:

> *There are so many empty houses in good areas and lots of homeless people selling the* Big Issue *– it doesn't make sense. Why can't they turn the empty houses into shared houses for young people, with worker support and self-contained flats for those who are ready for independent living.*

There was also a suggestion of the need for more bond deposit schemes to enable young people to access private flats.

PROFESSIONALS' VIEWS

We discuss the ideas put forward by professionals under two headings. First, we look at suggestions of early interventions to prevent or halt the incidence of running away. Then, we look at needs identified for young people who spend time away from home.

EARLY INTERVENTIONS

Many professionals recognised the need for preventative services and early interventions, even though they were working with young people who had passed the point when these would be effective. As one project worker put it:

> By the time they have got to us, it's not too late but a lot could have been done to stop them running away in the first place.

Their suggestions included:

- more help for parents who are experiencing difficulties with teenagers;

- recognising that parents who had had a difficult time with their own young people could be recruited to provide 'parent to parent' support;

- mediation services for families;

- the possible extension of family group conferences as a preventative measure. Short breaks from families, as a form of respite care, was also seen as a possible preventative measure.

There was also recognition of the contribution that schools could make through identifying early difficulties and by an exploration of these issues being part of the curriculum.

A recurring theme from many of the respondents was the need for young people to have someone who would listen to them, and who would be 'for them'. Their suggestions included:

- young person counselling services;

- young people's advocacy schemes;

- peer support networks;

- mentoring;

- telephone helplines.

There were specific concerns based on their experiences that social services may not be approached by young people who have had no previous contact. Also, that they were not organised to offer direct counselling services for young people who were beginning to have difficulties at home. Counselling services for young people under 12 were also suggested by some staff.

RESPONDING TO YOUNG PEOPLE WHO ARE AWAY FROM HOME

Several of the agency staff commented on the value of a 'quick response' facility when young people start running away. This may be a centre, refuge or safe house project with short-stay accommodation that provides an opportunity for 'independent' workers to explore the reasons for the young person's situation, assess the problems and attempt to respond to these. It was clear from our interviews that such facilities were generally in very short supply, resulting in many young people being returned to their families or care, often to similar problematic circumstances, and consequently to running away again.

The majority of professionals we interviewed worked with young people aged 16 and 17 who were 'on the streets'. It would be difficult to overstate the high degree of vulnerability of the young people and the demanding nature of this work. Our respondents frequently referred to these young people's physical and mental health needs, their drug and alcohol problems, and their high risk sexual behaviour:

> It is extremely difficult for young people to access the mental
> health service... we have a young people's unit in Newcastle
> which is based in the general hospital and young people have to
> be referred through their GP in order to access that service. The
> referral takes absolutely ages and for young people who are
> homeless they just have no concept of registering at the GP and...
> going through that process. There isn't an open access provision
> at all for mental health and then it takes very long even if they do
> know about it.

Suggestions were made in response to gaps in specific geographical localities. These included the need for young people to have information about services, for more 'drop in' centres, and for more retreats, night shelters, respite and emergency accommodation. In one city, there was a plea to stop cleansing the streets of homeless young people for festivals and civic occasions!

In a number of areas, the problems faced by young people leaving care were highlighted, including placement movement and disruption, poor practical preparation and lack of after-care support:

> There is a huge gap for those leaving care; most of them have very little in the way of living skills. Perhaps if there was more support at that stage, coming up to leaving care and then afterwards, and more provision for those young people in terms of accommodation they could be supported on an outreach basis.

Views were also expressed on the need for more staff training, particularly in relation to drug awareness, sexuality and sexual health issues.

Most of the workers we interviewed drew attention to the difficulties they had in accessing accommodation for 16- and 17-year-olds. Some of the young people they were working with were excluded from hostels because they were not working or because of drug and alcohol problems, and other young people, who had been evicted or had left with rent arrears, were unable to secure mainstream housing association or local authority tenancies.

In addition, many workers identified the low level of discretionary benefits, single room rent restrictions, and discretionary local authority housing and accommodation policies in respect of 16- and 17-year-olds, as major barriers to these young people accessing and securing affordable accommodation.

> There are so many rules and hoops that they have to jump through now as well. I mean in terms of their initial contact of making a claim, they now have to prove their identity and not many young people have a driver's licence, a passport or birth certificate, especially if they're homeless and they're that age range. Trying to get a birth certificate means having contact with the family that they don't want to have contact with.

As a consequence, many of these young people were trapped 'on the streets' unable to escape hostels, bed and breakfast, or street culture. Some of the hostels were seen by the staff we interviewed as inadequate, particularly if they contained a wide age range of people with drug, alcohol and mental health problems. There were suggestions for far smaller units.

Many of the workers we interviewed recognised the need for good quality housing plus support schemes, including 24-hour back-up support, as a way to assist these young people 'out of the streets'. Suggested models of support included direct work by dedicated staff, befriending schemes and mentoring:

There was a need for provision for those who don't want to live independently. Something like a community house where someone goes in and they are supported but can have a longer time there. Like two young people who have been with us for a while but I can't see it's going to work when they move out, they need two or three years more. Last year, a young woman did really well with us and she went out to another organisation, she was eventually evicted from there and went to another area and was evicted from there and is now on remand. She has mild cerebral palsy and she fought hard to achieve things but she wasn't capable of living on her own. There's a growing group of young people like that.

Concerns were voiced by some professionals about the failure to respond to the needs of black and Asian young people in their areas. Suggestions included the need for more ethnically sensitive services, including the appointment of black and Asian staff, targeted services and a greater understanding of cultural differences.

I believe that a lot of young people might not fit in with the existing services. For example, they might go to a rehab centre, or a refuge, they may go to any of these existing services and they will not fit in because their identity is different. So the existing services might not be able to cater for them completely and, if we have nothing else as back-up, what else is there for these young people?

Workers drew attention to the racism experienced by black and Asian young people in some hostels and their isolation in being offered accommodation in predominantly white areas. A project which worked with Asian young people had succeeded in developing coun-selling services, mediation, parenting workshops, a telephone helpline and a befriending scheme. It had developed strong links with the local community and most of the referrals were by word of mouth.

Workers in rural areas drew attention to the lack of information and advice for young people, transport restrictions, and the general short-age of affordable housing. Suggestions included the possibility of floating support and advice, or even a mobile van providing a place to stop overnight.

Finally, there were pleas for more inter-agency co-ordination. In some areas, there were many different types of projects – for drug abuse, young offenders, streetwork, young women, health – but a lack of co-ordination and overall strategic thinking and planning:

> *There needs to be a much more holistic view of an individual, particularly when I think they're coming out of care and looking at how you deal with all of their needs and develop a comprehensive service.*

CHAPTER 14

Policy and practice implications

In this final chapter of the report, we will draw together the key findings from the research and discuss the practice and policy challenges they raise. We begin with a summary of the key data from the study, presented in the order of the chapters of the report. We then go on to identify four key issues that emerge from the study in relation to young people who run away or are forced to leave. A range of appropriate practice responses are discussed before we examine the social policy implications of the findings.

SUMMARY

RUNNING AWAY/BEING FORCED TO LEAVE UNDER THE AGE OF 16

Prevalence and characteristics (Chapter 3)

- One in nine (11%) young people in the UK run away from home or are forced to leave and stay away overnight before the age of 16. This amounts to around 77,000 young people under 16 running away for the first time each year.

- Over half (54%) of young runaways only run away once but around one in eight (12%) run away more than three times. We estimate that there are around 129,000 incidents of young people running away over night each year in the UK.

- Around a fifth (19%) of these young people said they had been forced to leave home rather than run away.

- Prevalence rates are similar for different countries/types of areas.

- More females (11.5%) run away than males (8.5%).

- Rates for different ethnic groups are more similar than previous research suggested.

- Young people who start running away before the age of 11 are particularly likely to go on to run away repeatedly.

Triggers and contexts (Chapters 4 to 6)

- Problems at home are the primary reason for running away (mentioned by 80% of young runaways).

- There is a wide range of problems but family conflict is the most common.

- Over a quarter of young people run away due to physical abuse, emotional abuse and neglect.

- Other reasons for running away are of less significance, but the most important seem to be problems with peers (8%) and problems at school (8%).

- Young people who live in step-families or with a lone parent are significantly more likely to run away (21% and 13% respectively) than those living with both birth parents (7%).

- Young people who ran away had significantly more negative views of the quality of their relationship with their parents. For example, being hit a lot and not being treated fairly were both much more common amongst runaways (10% and 34% of runaways respectively mentioned these two problems).

- Professionals concurred with the findings from the survey that poor family relationships make running away more likely irrespective of family form. However, there are additional stresses of living in families where changes in form have taken place which also make running away more likely.

- Young people who run away repeatedly have particularly high levels of family disruption and problems.

- Young people who are currently living in substitute care are much more likely to have run away (45%) than young people living with their family (10%).

- Young people's reasons for running away from care included wanting to return home and unhappiness about the decisions being made about them.

- In the interview sample, half of the young people who had run away before the age of 16 had spent some time living in substitute care. However, they had generally started running away before living in substitute care, and the period they had spent in care was often a relatively small proportion of their lives.

- Young people who run away are more likely than average to have other problems in their lives, including problems with depression (55%), alcohol (25%), drugs (19%), offending (21%), peer relationships and at school.

- The survey found little evidence of a direct link between economic factors and running away.

- Most of the young people we interviewed who had not lived in substitute care had had no assistance from agencies with the problems they were experiencing before they first ran away.

Experiences and patterns of being away (Chapter 7)

- The majority of young people (84%) remain in their local area when they run away.

- The experience of being away had both negative and positive aspects. Many young people felt that they had had time to think (83%) and relief from pressure (65%) whilst away. However, many felt lonely (39%), hungry (23%) or frightened (32%), and a large minority had faced risks such as sleeping rough (25%) and being physically or sexually assaulted whilst away (15%).

- The majority of young people rely on friends and relatives for support whilst away, but around one in seven (14%) relied solely on more risky strategies, including stealing, begging, and survival sex.

- Most young people (70%) return home of their own accord.

- There is no evidence of a difference in running-away experiences according to the age when they happen.

- For young people who run away more than once, there is little evidence of a coherent, consistent or developing pattern in young

people's experiences whilst away from home.
- Young people who run away repeatedly do appear to have different experiences (i.e. face more risks) than young people who only run away once or twice. These tendencies are often in evidence from the first time young people run away.

Sub-groups of young people (Chapter 8)

- The research has identified four broad groups of young people who run away: young people who do not run away overnight, those who run away overnight once or twice, those who run away overnight repeatedly, and those who become detached for lengthy periods.

- Generally, young people face greater risks and problems where running away is more repetitive and/or lengthy.

- However, the issues faced by young people in all four of the above groups point to the need for a range of interventions.

YOUNG PEOPLE WHO SPEND TIME AWAY AT AGES 16 AND 17
Prevalence and characteristics (Chapter 9)

- The data gathered from professionals indicates that there is a substantial prevalence of young people aged 16 and 17 being away from home in unstable situations.

- This incidence tends to be more hidden in rural areas than in suburban and city areas.

- There is a significant incidence of being away amongst African-Caribbean and Asian young people but this also tends to be mostly hidden due to fears of racism and lack of appropriate services.

Triggers and contexts (Chapter 10)

- The family context of young people who first spent time away at 16 or 17 differed from those who had run away under 16, with less evidence of overt abuse.

- The most common trigger for leaving home amongst this older age group was family conflict, and there was a substantial incidence of this leading to young people being forced to leave home by their parents.

- Relatively few of the young people who had not run away before the age of 16 had spent any time in substitute care.

- The significance of peer relationships as a contributory factor to leaving home seems much less pronounced for young people over the age of 16 than for younger teenagers.

- Issues relating to mental health, alcohol and drugs were prevalent amongst young people who first left home at 16 or 17, although offending was perhaps less of an issue.

- Experiences of school were more positive for young people who started being away at 16 or 17 than for younger runaways.

- Economic factors within families due to current benefits and housing policies seem to be an important contributory factor leading to some young people in this age group being forced to leave home.

Experiences and patterns of being away (Chapter 11)

- Most of the young people interviewed who had spent time away at 16 or 17, had experience of running away or being forced to leave before the age of 16.

- There seems to be a significant incidence of young people being forced to leave home at the ages of 16 and 17, often due to family conflict.

- There was evidence of risky experiences and survival strategies for this age group.

- Young people who spent time away at this age often turned to agencies for help and support, and there is evidence of positive usage of both statutory and voluntary services.

- There is evidence of several different patterns at 16 and 17, with some young people who spend time away attempting to return home, often only to face the same problems again, others gaining access to emergency and longer-term accommodation, and some remaining detached and living 'on the streets'.

Sub-groups (Chapter 12)

- Young people who had started running away at a younger age had significantly higher levels of detachment at 16 and 17 than those who started older.

VIEWS ON WHAT COULD BE DIFFERENT

Both the young people and professionals identified a wide range of potential interventions with young people who run away or are forced to leave home.

Views of young people (Chapter 13)

- Young people's suggestions for preventative work included family support and mediation services, advice and counselling services and school-based services.

- In terms of young people under 16 being away from home, the young people identified the need for more emergency accommodation accessible to this age group and also more accessible advice and support.

- Similarly, in terms of 16- and 17-year-olds, young people felt that the key needs were more supported accommodation and better advice and support services.

- Generally, in all of the above contexts, young people also identified the need for improved information about what services are available.

Views of professionals (Chapter 13)

- Professionals suggested the need for early interventions involving more support for parents, family mediation services and youth counselling services.

- The need for quick response facilities for young people who had started running away under the age of 16 was identified.

- For the 16 to 17 age group, the main suggestions of professionals were a better range and availability of supported accommodation, changes to the benefits rules, ongoing support for young people, and better inter-agency co-ordination.

- The need for more ethnically sensitive services and improved services in rural areas were also highlighted by professionals.

KEY ISSUES FROM THE RESEARCH

From our summary, we highlight four key issues which we feel are particularly central to an understanding of the needs of young people who run away or are forced to leave home, and the formulation of appropriate practice and social policy responses.

THE SCALE OF THE PROBLEM

The research has clearly demonstrated that running away or being forced to leave home is a widespread phenomenon amongst young people under the age of 18. This is true for all four countries of the UK; for rural, suburban and city areas; and for all sub-groups of young people (although there is some variation by gender and ethnicity).

FAMILY PROBLEMS

Young people run away primarily from problems within the family, and the research has highlighted three key issues here:

- the incidence of abuse within families as a factor leading to many young people running away;

- the impact on young people of family breakdown and the reconstitution of families, increasing their likelihood of running away;

- the incidence of young people being forced to leave home during their teenage years.

RISKS AND SURVIVAL

Young people away from home face risks of hunger, fear, loneliness and are vulnerable to being hurt or exploited by others. These risks are in evidence not only for those who sleep rough but also for those who stay with relatives and strangers.

Young people away from home often lack legitimate means of survival and some resort to strategies such as begging, stealing, and using drugs and alcohol.

Some young people who run away become detached and excluded from their families, their schools and their communities. Young people who start running away before the age of 11 are particularly vulnerable in this respect.

PRACTICE RESPONSES

Our schools survey and our interviews with young people carry important messages for policy and practice. To begin with, they point to two guiding principles: first, the need to listen to the young person's viewpoint – to explore and see the world as they do; second, to understand running away within the context of young people's lives – their heritage and ethnicity, their experiences of family, community, school, friendships, substitute care, and other agencies and networks that they encounter.

The research has highlighted the high incidence of running away, the diverse characteristics of the young people, the different situations from which they run away, and the variety of pathways and experiences. Such diversity suggests a range of policy and practice interventions. A model which is relevant to the exploration of policy and practice implications arising from our present study identifies primary, secondary and tertiary interventions, and has been developed from earlier research work (Stein *et al.*, 1994).

PRIMARY INTERVENTION (PREVENTATIVE WORK)

Primary interventions are those that focus upon preventative work with all young people and their families within the community. The high incidence of running away and the experiences of young people outlined in this research point to the need for widespread discussion of this issue. Our research found that one in nine (11%) young people run away from home or are forced to leave before the age of 16. This is the same for England, Scotland, Wales and Northern Ireland; for rural, suburban and city areas; and broadly similar irrespective of gender, ethnicity and economic status.

In schools, the issue of young people 'running away' could be a compulsory topic within the personal and social education

curriculum. Perhaps, as our young people suggested, this could be as part of a wider exploration of family relationships and planning for adult life. This would not only increase general awareness of the issue among young people – the next generation of parents – it may also encourage young people who are thinking of running away to seek help.

Also, given the present Government's commitment to the importance of early prevention for combating social exclusion and marginalisation, the issue could be part of parenting preparation programmes. In this context, the focus could be on positive child-centred parenting – listening, involving and engaging children and young people in families.

Different types of television and radio programmes, articles in young people's magazines, storylines in 'soaps', poster campaigns and leaflets in places that young people use, clearly identifying sources of help, may all, for example, contribute to a greater awareness of the subject.

SECONDARY INTERVENTION

Secondary interventions are directed at young people who start running away during the daytime or have run away overnight once or twice. These interventions aim at preventing an established pattern of running-away behaviour and detachment from family and substitute care.

As our survey has clearly demonstrated, most young people first run away from the family. Our findings also indicate that young people would have welcomed the opportunity to talk to someone at the time, someone who would listen to them and help them. But for most of our young people, this 'quick response' accessible service was lacking – they were unaware or felt unable to use existing services, or such services did not exist. There was evidence that young people who had no previous contact with social services were unlikely to approach them, and some of those who had a social worker wanted more time with them.

There is a strong case for every young person who runs away to be offered an interview in order to assess the reasons and risks and agree a response. The initial interview should be with someone who can engage the young person and in whom they feel they can confide. A confidential school-, further-education or youth-based counselling service, complemented by peer counselling and telephone helplines may all help in identifying initial problems. For many young people, this first response may be enough to resolve the situation.

However, as our research suggests, there may be a significant minority for whom running away is an escape from feeling neglected at home, violent verbal confrontations, or abuse. Over a quarter of the young people surveyed ran away due to physical abuse, emotional abuse or neglect. Our survey also showed that young people who ran away had significantly more negative views of the quality of their relationships with their parents – for example being hit a lot and not being treated fairly. They also had high levels of family disruption. This is most likely to be in reconstituted families and involve conflicts with step-parents. Outside the family, young people are most likely to be experiencing difficulties at school or problems with peers and we had clear evidence of bullying.

Against this background, their running away could initially be regarded as a positive action; removing themselves from an abusive situation. The young people also reported that they had time to think and relief from pressure whilst away. However, many felt lonely hungry or frightened, and a large minority faced risks such as sleeping rough and being physically and/or sexually assaulted whilst away. The majority of these young people relied on friends and relatives for support, but around one in seven used more risky strategies including stealing, begging and survival sex. Most returned home of their own accord.

In these circumstances, it is important that the initial assessment is followed up by some positive action and the young person is not simply returned to the same circumstances which precipitated them running away. This may include direct work with the family and the young person in addressing the issues which led to the young person running away. We would strongly support the view, expressed by both young people and professionals, that there is a need to help families to address their problems. **Mediation services, parent-to-parent counselling, family group conferencing and respite care may all contribute to this end. Responding to the needs of under-11s who run away is clearly highlighted by the findings of the research.**

There should also be early attempts to solve any problems which have arisen at school. Truancy, exclusion, and difficulties in learning are all warning bells for running away.

Although there is the legislative framework within England, Scotland, Wales and Northern Ireland to provide services to young people and their families, our research would suggest that there is a gap in the provision of this direct work and thus a failure to intervene at a stage which may prevent further episodes of running away.

TERTIARY INTERVENTION

Tertiary interventions focus on work with young people 'on the streets'; those who become detached from family or care after running away. Some of these types of intervention have been established in some major cities by The Children's Society and other organisations.

Our findings reveal that young people on the streets may include two main groups of young people. First, those young people with an established history of running away. Typically, they are likely to begin running away from violence, abuse or neglect, most often within a reconstituted family. They may return, or be returned, to the family home on many occasions with little or no attempt to address the reasons for running away. They are also likely to have problems such as truanting from school, offending and may have other problems, including depression, and alcohol and drug abuse. They may also spend some time in substitute care. Our survey showed that young people who are currently living in substitute care are much more likely to run away than young people living within the family and, in our interview sample, half of the young people who had run away before the age of 16 had spent some time in substitute care. However, the latter group had generally started running away before living in care, and the period they had spent in care was often a relatively small proportion of their lives.

The second group of young people are those who are thrown out by their families, or who have decided they have had enough and leave before they are evicted, most often at around 16 or 17 years of age. Family conflict, including deteriorating relationships, often with a step-parent, is most likely to precipitate their running away. Some of these young people have not run away before or had experience of substitute care or life 'on the streets'. Mental health, alcohol and drug problems were prevalent among young people who first left home at

16 or 17. However, most of the 16- and 17-year-old young people we interviewed had previously run away or been forced to leave home before the age of 16.

For both of these groups, their experience of life 'on the streets' includes sleeping rough, drifting, going hungry, loneliness, fear, verbal abuse and physical and sexual assaults – a continuation of the exploitation and victimisation that began within the family. Their survival strategies include stealing, begging, using drugs and alcohol, and providing sex for money or accommodation. Perhaps not surprisingly, our interviews with both young people and professionals highlighted the instability of their lives and revealed both physical and mental health problems. Our interviews with professionals also suggested that the incidence was more hidden in rural areas than in suburban and city areas, and that there was a significant incidence of being away amongst African-Caribbean and Asian young people, but this also tends to be hidden due to fears of racism and a lack of appropriate services.

Tertiary interventions identified in our research include refuges, drop-in centres, youth work projects and street-based outreach work, such as those piloted by The Children's Society. What these different approaches have in common is their engagement with young people in a way that was often seen by them as very positive. Young people found them sensitive to the harm they had suffered and responsive to their needs to build on their adult survival strengths – in contrast to more punitive policies which re-victimised them and ineffective attempts to return them to abusive situations.

For young people aged 16 and 17, drop-in centres, refuges, supported hostels and outreach work were able to provide much needed practical support and advice as well as help some of them to develop safer survival strategies. Youth-work projects were able to help some other young people move into their own accommodation, find employment, further education or training, and establish independent lives. Young people voiced the need for more information about services, provision of smaller hostels and more safe places to go at night.

In addition, a small number of very young people, aged 11–15, become detached from their families or care. Refuge work attempts where possible to negotiate a return. However, as suggested earlier, this may prove unsatisfactory if the young person is simply being returned to the same risks of confrontation, abuse and neglect within the family, or to what they regard as similar problems in their care placement.

Our interviews with professionals suggest there is a need for more ethnically sensitive services to respond to the needs of black and Asian young people. They drew attention to the need for more black and Asian staff, more targeted services and a greater understanding of cultural differences. A project which worked well with Asian young people – offering counselling, befriending, mediation, parenting workshops and telephone helplines – had succeeded by developing strong links with the local community.

Our interviews with professionals in rural areas highlighted the lack of information and advice, transport restrictions, and the general shortage of emergency accommodation.

SOCIAL POLICY ISSUES

Our research findings also raise a number of broader social policy issues.

FAMILY POLICY

Our survey, consistent with earlier research findings, found that the rate of running away is significantly higher amongst young people living with a lone parent and step-parent than amongst young people living with both parents (Rees, 1993). Our survey findings and interviews with young people reveal that many young people in reconstituted families run away having experienced violence, abuse or having reported feeling neglected within the family.

Currently, one in twelve children live in step-parent families, and increasing numbers of young people are experiencing family breakdown. Parenting support and assisting families are high policy priorities of the present Government as exemplified by the Green Paper *Supporting Families* (1998), the setting up of the National Family and Parenting Institute, the provision of Parenting Orders under the Crime and Disorder Act 1998, and the Sure Start under 5 initiative. In addition, many statutory and voluntary agencies are offering Family Support services – under Section 17 of the Children Act 1989 in England and Wales, under Section 22 of the Children (Scotland) Act 1995 and

Articles 17 and 18 of the Children (Northern Ireland) Order 1995.

However, much of the focus of existing work is on under-8s, where there are major child protection concerns. **What 'older' young people need is someone who can engage and listen to them, attempt to ensure their needs are met when adults separate, and be available for them and their families to help resolve problems which may arise. In short, this age group of young people need to be more visible in family social policy.** For young people who run away, this could be facilitated by the development of primary, secondary and tertiary services as outlined earlier. It may also be progressed by young people being more involved in decisions which affect their lives, as discussed below (see Young people under 16).

SUBSTITUTE CARE

Completed research studies have shown that young people 'looked after' by local authority social services departments are over-represented among young people who run away. Surveys have found that, while less than 1% of children are looked after, around 30% of young runaways reported to the police are missing from substitute care, the vast majority from residential care. Studies of refuges and street-work projects have also found that young people from substitute care are over-represented among young runaways (see Biehal, 1998, for a summary of research findings). There is considerable variation in numbers missing from residential care. A recent study (Wade *et al.*, 1998) found that the proportion of 11- to 16-year-olds accommodated in children's homes during one year who went missing overnight, or were reported missing to the police at least once, ranged from around 25% in two local authorities to 65–71% in another two.

Although the main purpose of our schools survey was to investigate young people running away from the family, it did show that young people in care were over-represented amongst young people who run away and that most of these young people had first run away while living at home. The results of our interviews with young people add to this picture. Overall, we as researchers formed the view that care had generally failed to compensate them for their pre-care experiences. It failed to provide secure attachments, stability, educational success, and prepare and support them in their transition to adulthood. The consequence of this is that many found themselves 'on the streets'.

Although a detailed exploration of running away from care was beyond the scope of this research, we would endorse the findings from Wade *et al.*'s major study. **There is an urgent need to improve the quality of substitute foster and residential care, increase placement choice, particularly the expansion of professional fostering, and generally improve outcomes for children and young people living in and leaving substitute care.** In this context, the Quality Protects programme provides a general framework for developing services (Department of Health, 1998).

There is also a need to develop more strategic responses to running away through central monitoring and the identification of placements with high rates of running away, to provide more guidance and advice to staff, and develop better inter-agency co-ordination. *The Government's Response to the Children's Safeguards Review* (Department of Health, 1998) and the joint guidance on the action to be taken when a child goes missing from care, drawn up by the Local Government Association and the Association of Chief Police Officers (ACPO,1997), has promised new statutory guidance. *The Government's Response* states:

> *It is particularly important that, whenever a child returns, or is returned by others, a full assessment should be made of the reasons why the incident occurred and whether the child's placement remains suitable. Accurate records must be maintained of every incident, and senior managers should examine the reasons why children have gone missing and any variations in the rate at which they run away from different children's homes and foster carers.* (p.16)

The Response also states:

> *The Government also recognises the importance of refuges which cater for young people. It will work constructively with local government and voluntary bodies to strengthen their role and financial basis.* (p.16)

New arrangements for young people leaving care are also promised and have been detailed in the consultation paper *Me, Survive Out There?* (Department of Health, 1999).

YOUNG PEOPLE UNDER 16

Both our questionnaire and interview sample revealed that there were young people under 16 who had become detached from their families and care, some for more than six months. As a sub-sample, they represent the most vulnerable group of young people. They possess no legal status, as they should be living with someone who has parental responsibility or be looked after by the local authority, and as such they have no service entitlements whilst 'on the streets'. In effect, they are 'non-citizens'.

As our research has shown, they become detached from their families, foster carers and children's homes, as well as their schools and local communities. Their survival strategies involve serious risks to themselves and to others. Some of the young people we interviewed testified to the effectiveness of different forms of tertiary interventions. However, we were generally struck by the failure of earlier interventions to respond effectively to their problems, and, in particular, the views of many young people that they were not listened to or heard.

It is significant to note that there is no legal requirement in England, Wales and Northern Ireland for parents to take into account children's views in reaching any decisions (except where they are 'looked after' or are in dispute proceedings under the Children Act 1989). This is in contrast to Section 6 of the Children (Scotland) Act 1995. **A change in the law to require parents to consider children and young people's 'wishes and feelings', with regard to a child's age and maturity, would be consistent with a more child-centred approach and comply more fully with Article 12 of the United Nations Convention on the Rights of the Child.**

Also, given the strong link between truancy and running away, schools have an important contribution to make in both preventing and responding to running away. Primary and secondary preventative measures such as curriculum topics and school-based counselling services have been outlined earlier. **In addition, there is a need to reduce the risk of disaffection among young people and, in this context, the Government's guidance on *Social Inclusion: Pupil Support* (Department of Education and Employment, 1999) is to be welcomed.** It is based on existing examples of good practice and its key principles, particularly early interventions, supporting behaviour management, working with parents, involving pupils (for example, in anti-bullying and harassment policies, and school councils), commitment to equal opportunities and identifying underlying causes, all offer constructive responses.

YOUNG PEOPLE AGED 16 AND 17

Earlier research has shown that youth homelessness is strongly associated with past experiences of foster and residential care, child protection as well as family conflict, step-parenting and violence or abuse within the family. Research from the USA has also identified a link between established patterns or careers of running away and later youth homelessness (Simons and Whitbeck, 1991). Our findings are consistent with these and thus point to the importance of early interventions.

There is also research evidence that young single people are over-represented among the single homeless and are disadvantaged in systems which determine access to social housing. They are also more likely than other young people to suffer from psychiatric disorders and have a high rate of self-reported health problems (Pleace and Quilgars, 1999).

For young people aged 16 and 17 who are unable to return home, many of the projects aim to help them to establish independent lives by assisting them to find accommodation and employment, further education or training, or secure financial support. However, as many project workers reported, their efforts are often frustrated by the present legislative framework, resulting in many young people drifting from hostels and night shelters to sleeping rough 'on the streets'.

As the law currently stands, single homeless young people aged 16–17 are not automatically accepted under the homelessness legislation in England, Wales and Northern Ireland, despite income support for this age group being abolished in 1988. The exception to this is Scotland, where young people under 21 who are 'looked after' by a local authority at school-leaving age or later, are accepted as being in priority need.

The 1991 Code of Guidance for England and Wales suggested that local authorities may accept young people 'at risk', but that 16- and 17-year-olds should not be accepted as being vulnerable on the basis of their age alone (Section 6. 13, DoE, 1991). Some local authorities have used their discretionary powers to accept young people, whilst others have interpreted their duties in a more restrictive way. Recent research by Anderson and Morgan (1997) showed that over half of local authorities usually or always awarded priority to 16- and 17-year-olds leaving care and young people referred under the Children Act 1989, but less than a quarter accepted young people on the basis of their age alone.

The Children Act 1989 gave social services departments the duty, working alongside housing authorities and other agencies, to provide accommodation for 'any child in need in their area who has reached the age of 16 and whose welfare that authority considers likely to be seriously prejudiced if they do not provide accommodation' (Section 20(3)). However, as with the homelessness legislation, the interpretation of 'in need' has varied and many social services have not regarded homelessness as sufficient reason to trigger their responsibilities.

In response to the Social Exclusion Unit's report on rough sleeping, the Department of the Environment, Transport and the Regions has issued a consultation document as a basis for revising the 1991 Code of Guidance. **It is proposed that care leavers and homeless 16- and 17-year-olds without 'back-up support' should be accepted as 'vulnerable' by housing authorities under the homelessness legislation (Social Exclusion Unit, 1998). Our research would point to the urgent need for such a policy response.**

Also, many of the workers we interviewed highlighted the problems for young people surviving on the low level of benefits for under 25-year-olds. They also voiced their concerns about the impact of the single-room restrictions on the quality and availability of property to rent.

Our interviews with young people and project workers also highlighted the difficulties experienced by young people 'on the streets', without a job or training place, in claiming severe hardship payments. Payments of this allowance is short-term (6 or 8 weeks), discretionary and the Guidance requires confirmation of evidence provided from the young person by a parent or, where abuse is alleged, by a 'responsible third party'. Many of the young people we interviewed are deterred and resort to begging and other survival strategies. There is a strong case for reviewing access to benefits for estranged 16/17-year-olds.

Financial assistance to care leavers in the four nations is also discretionary, leading to considerable variation in financial support.

INTER-AGENCY RESPONSE

Our survey of 13,000 young people, our interviews with professionals and with young people themselves have clearly highlighted the number of different agencies who may become involved in the lives of young people who run away. Police, social services, education, youth services, voluntary agencies, health, youth justice, drug and alcohol projects, housing associations and authorities, as well as dedicated services for street children and young people who run away, may, at some point, become involved. Perhaps not surprisingly, there were pleas from professionals for more inter-agency co-ordination, and in some areas there were successful examples of multi-agency forums.

We would argue strongly for the need for joint strategies between the police, social services and voluntary agencies when young people run away either from care (as detailed in the procedures issued by the Local Government Association and the Association of Chief Police Officers (1997), or from the family home.

In addition, there is a clear need for more systematic information and recording of running away, and improved co-ordination at a corporate level, so that different types of projects and agencies work together to an agreed local strategy. This process should be enabled by local authorities who are required to include in their Children's Services Plans information about services for young runaways who find themselves homeless and without support.

CHALLENGING SOCIAL EXCLUSION

This research presents a number of challenges. First of all, where appropriate, to prevent young people from becoming detached from their families, schools and communities by persistently running away. Second, to intervene effectively in the lives of young people already 'on the streets'. As this research powerfully demonstrates through the voices of young people themselves, the consequences of failing to meet these challenges include unacceptable risks. Fear, loneliness, hunger, and verbal, physical and sexual assaults combine with begging, stealing, drug use and prostitution to make survival on the streets dangerous and distressing. And this often follows a pattern of exploitation and victimisation within their own families from which they have run away or been thrown out. At just 16 and 17, many of these young people are likely to be homeless, 'status zero' and 'off register' young people – outside education, training or employment – their life chances severely blighted with enormous costs to themselves and society.

To challenge the social exclusion of this small but significant minority of young people, we have proposed a series of primary, secondary and tertiary interventions. We have also recommended social policy changes. However, there is a final, more fundamental challenge, not only to policy makers and those agencies working with young people who run away, but to society as a whole. It became evident to us as researchers, interviewing young people and reading what they had written about their lives, how far as a society we still have to go to listen, to hear, to understand and to respond effectively and sensitively in meeting their needs.

References

Abrahams C and Mungal R (1992) *Young Runaways: Exploding the Myths*. London: NCH Action for Children.

Adams J (1996) 'Bridging the gap.' Plymouth: Youth Enquiry Service.

Anderson I and Morgan J (1997) *Social Housing for Single People? A Study of Local Policy and Practice*. Stirling: University of Stirling.

Barter C (1996) *Nowhere to Hide: Giving Young Runaways a Voice*. London: Centrepoint/NSPCC.

Biehal N (1998) *Young Runaways. Highlights* No. 164. London: National Children's Bureau.

Brennan T, Huizinga D and Elliott D (1978) *The Social Psychology of Runaways*. New York: Lexington Books.

Carlin L and Bradstreet S (1999) *The RSI in Glasgow: Monitoring Report*, March 1999. Glasgow: Glasgow Council for Single Homeless.

Centrepoint (1998) *The Young Face of Homelessness* (Youth Affairs Briefing – December 1998). London: Centrepoint.

Department for Education and Employment (1999) *Social Inclusion: Pupil Support*. Circular number 10/99. London: Department for Education and Employment Publications.

Department of Health (1999) *Me, Survive Out There? New Arrangements for Young People Living in and Leaving Care*. London: Department of Health.

Department of Health (1998) *The Government's Response to the Children's Safeguards Review*. Cm 4105. London: The Stationery Office.

Department of Health (1998) *The Quality Protects Programme: Transforming Children's Services*, LAC(98) 28. London: Department of Health.

Galvin G, Steele A and Somerville P (undated) *Single Homelessness in Salford*. Salford: University of Salford, Department of Environmental Health and Housing.

Gunner J, Tod T and Pollard A (1997) *Young People's Housing Options in Devon*. London: Centrepoint.

Gwynedd Council (1998) *Rough Sleeping: 1998 Update*. Caernarfon: Gwynedd Council.

Home Office (1998) *Supporting Families*. London: The Stationery Office.

Hutson S and Jones S (1997) *Rough Sleeping and Homelessness in Rhondda Cynon Taff*. University of Glamorgan.

Local Government Association and the Association of Chief Police Officers (1997) *Missing from Care: Procedures and Practices in Caring for Missing Children*. London: Local Government Association.

Newman C (1989) *Young Runaways: Findings from Britain's first Safe House*. London: The Children's Society.

Office for Population Censuses and Surveys (1994) *1991 Census: Key Statistics for Local Authorities – Great Britain*. London: HMSO.

Pleace N and Quilgars D (1999) 'Youth homelessness' in Rugg J (ed.) *Young People and Housing*. London: Routledge.

Rees G (1993) *Hidden Truths: Young People's Experiences of Running Away*. London: The Children's Society.

Rees G and Stein M (forthcoming) *The Abuse of Adolescents within the Family*. London: NSPCC.

Shelter Cymru (1997) *Rough Sleepers: A Rural Issue?* Wrexham: Shelter Cymru.

Simons R and Whitbeck L (1991) 'Running away during adolescence as a precursor to adult homelessness.' *Social Services Review*, volume 65 (2), pages 224–247, June 1991.

Social Exclusion Unit (1998) *Rough Sleeping Report*, Cm 4008. London: HMSO.

Stein M, Rees G and Frost N (1994) *Running – the Risk: Young People on the Streets of Britain Today*. London: The Children's Society.

Utting, Sir William (1997) *People Like Us: The Report of the Review of the Safeguards for Children Living Away from Home*. London: The Stationery Office.

Wade J and Biehal N with Clayden J and Stein M (1998) *Going Missing: Young People Absent from Care*. Chichester: John Wiley and Sons.

Wilkinson M with Craig G (1998) *Single Homelessness in the Ashfield District of Nottinghamshire*. Hull: Policy Studies Research Centre, University of Lincolnshire and Humberside.

THE CHILDREN'S SOCIETY
A POSITIVE FORCE FOR CHANGE

The Children's Society is one of Britain's leading charities for children and young people. Founded in 1881 as a Christian organisation, The Children's Society reaches out unconditionally to children and young people regardless of race, culture or creed.

Over 90 projects throughout England and Wales
We work with over 30,000 children of all ages, focusing on those whose circumstances have made them particularly vulnerable. We aim to help stop the spiral into isolation, anger and lost hope faced by so many young people.

We constantly look for effective, new ways of making a real difference
We measure local impact and demonstrate through successful practice that major issues can be tackled and better resolved. The Children's Society has an established track record of taking effective action: both in changing public perceptions about difficult issues such as child prostitution, and in influencing national policy and practice to give young people a better chance at life.

The Children's Society is committed to overcoming injustice wherever we find it
We are currently working towards national solutions to social isolation, lack of education and the long-term problems they cause, through focused work in several areas:

- helping parents whose babies and toddlers have inexplicably stopped eating, endangering their development;
- involving children in the regeneration of poorer communities;
- preventing exclusions from primary and secondary schools;
- providing a safety net for young people who run away from home and care;
- seeking viable alternatives to the damaging effects of prison for young offenders.

The Children's Society will continue to raise public awareness of difficult issues to promote a fairer society for the most vulnerable children in England and Wales. For further information about the work of The Children's Society or to obtain a publications catalogue, please contact:
The Children's Society, Publishing Department, Edward Rudolf House, Margery Street, London WC1X 0JL. Tel. 0207 841 4400. Fax 0207 841 4500.

The Children's Society is a registered charity: Charity Registration No. 221124.